THE SECOND LONDON BAPTIST CONFESSION OF 1689

INCLUDES THE BAPTIST CATECHISM

THE SECOND LONDON BAPTIST CONFESSION OF 1689

INCLUDES THE BAPTIST CATECHISM

The National Center for Family-Integrated Churches
WAKE FOREST, NORTH CAROLINA

OTHER BOOKS
—— From the NCFIC ——

A Weed in the Church

Building a God-Centered Family

Family Reformation

Feminine by Design

Preparing Boys for Battle

Helping Them to Choose

It Can Be Done

Preparing for Marriage

Moment of Courage

Reunited Bible Study Challenge

The National Center for Family-Integrated Churches
220 S. White Street, Wake Forest, NC 27587
www.NCFIC.org

ISBN-10: 0-9851408-1-6
ISBN-13: 978-0-9851408-1-6

Cover Design By: Justin Turley
Book Design By: Tyler Dorin

PRINTED IN THE UNITED STATES OF AMERICA

THIS IS DEDICATED TO ALL THOSE FAMILIES AND
CHURCHES WHO DESIRE TO KNOW THEIR GOD AND SOW
THE SEEDS OF THE GOSPEL THROUGHOUT THE EARTH.
MAY YOU BE LIKE THOSE SPOKEN OF IN DANIEL: "THE
PEOPLE WHO KNOW THEIR GOD SHALL BE STRONG, AND
CARRY OUT GREAT EXPLOITS" (DAN. 11:32).

TABLE OF — CONTENTS —

— REPRINT — INFORMATION

The text for this version of the confession and its appendages "has been transcribed from a microfilm copy of an original 1677 [Second London Baptist] Confession,"[a] with some minor modifications (as described below). The original, non-edited version is attainable online. Some of the modifications, in this book, include (but are not limited to) the following: updating older English spellings of words; modifying some grammar, including word use, capitalizations, and punctuations; and adding some headings. In addition, some Scripture references have been added, removed, or modified.

The Baptist Catechism and associated text(s) are primarily drawn from an 1809 version of the catechism. This text has been preserved in its original form, in this book, with minor modifications, including (but not limited to) the following: modification of some grammar, including capitalizations, punctuations, and spelling, and slight modification of some Scripture references.* Some of the appendages after the catechism are from an 1851 version of the catechism.

*With permission, some Scripture references were used from the following website: http://www.reformedreader.org/ccc/bapcat.htm

INTRODUCTION
—— By Scott T. Brown ——

This confession is a deep mine, filled with the everlasting treasures of redemption. It reveals God to us. It helps us to think like Christians. It summarizes vast resources of wisdom from heaven. This is why the Second London Baptist Confession of 1689 is a wonderful resource for churches and families. There is no greater blessing to the human soul, to the family, to the church, and to the state than when minds are filled up with the riches of the knowledge of God.

A Strategic Purpose

In the introduction to this confession, the authors appeal to heads of households to teach these things of sound doctrine to their families. In the following section entitled "Letter to the Reader," you will notice how they appeal to "begin at home" and to remember that so much "decay of religion" can be traced to a father's neglect of family worship and instruction. They condemn heads of families who do not train, instruct, and catechize. They warn that their children's blood will be on their hands. This is why the authors of this confession intended that it be a tool to be used in families. The authors of this confession clearly understood and promoted the role of the family in upholding sound doctrine. God has given these confessions of faith, not only to churches and individuals, but also to families to use to instruct children in sound doctrine. Our prayer is that your family will enjoy many happy hours of learning, growing, and rejoicing in the wisdom of God that springs from every sentence of this confession.

A Time of Doctrinal Confusion

We live in a time of doctrinal confusion. Even a basic knowledge of God, as displayed in this confession, is unknown to most Christians. The average churchgoer seems completely disconnected from clear thinking about God. As a result church people are fuzzy on the Gospel and brain dead on the Law. This confession clears the confusion.

Basic Theology?

Most people alive today would consider this confession a course in advanced theology. On the contrary, when it was penned, it was thought to be a basic theology that even children could understand. This shows how far we have slipped in modern times, and it should wake us up to the urgency of bringing the whole counsel of God to the rising generation.

How Important Are Confessions?

It is critical to determine the importance of confessions. Confessions are not equivalent to the Bible, nor do they take the place of it. Rather, they systematize the overall teaching of the Bible in an orderly fashion in order to answer various questions that Christians need to have answered.

Scripture is the foundation of all doctrine, and the Second London Baptist Confession has its foundation in Scripture alone. Paul declares that "all Scripture is given by inspiration of God, and is profitable for doctrine, for reproof, for correction, for instruction in righteousness" (2 Tim. 3:16). What you find in the confession is an exposition of Scripture on the categories that it presents. Confessions are simply summaries of "sound words" spoken of in 2 Timothy 1:13-14. Paul says, "Hold fast the pattern of sound words." One way we do that is by explaining them in confessional form.

Protection from Fads and Movements

This confession has proven its value in the fact that it is a time-tested creed. It's not new. Why is that important? One reason is we're part of a flow of history. When we come up with our own creeds, we're saying that we're doing something new. We're saying that we're striking out on our own, when in fact, we really ought to be appealing to historic Christian doctrine. Enduring doctrinal statements are very important, because they keep us from fads and movements. They protect us from being "carried about with every wind of doctrine" (Eph. 4:14).

Who Embraced This Confession?

While this was the confession of Baptist Puritans, it did not die with them. It was embraced by preachers like Charles H. Spurgeon, John Bunyan, John Gill; theologians like John A. Broadus and B. H. Carroll; Baptist missionaries like William Carey, Adoniram Judson, Luther Rice, and Lottie Moon; Southern Baptist founders like Basil Manly, Sr., W. B. Johnson, R. B. C. Howell, P. H. Mell, James P. Boyce, and John L. Dagg. When you embrace this confession, you join the ranks of a long line of saints who have embraced this confession.

How Important Is Doctrinal Knowledge?

It would be a mistake to think that all we have to do is know the facts contained in this confession. Knowing doctrine should never be an end in itself, but rather, a means to an end. But does that mean that knowledge should not be a goal? Of course not! Knowledge should also be a goal. Just because knowledge is not the ultimate end does not mean that it should not be a goal. We should set ourselves to the goal of knowing God.

Sound Doctrine Can Be Useless

The modern church suffers from such a severe case of doctrine phobia that there are many who consider doctrine to be useless. There are many reasons people are afraid of doctrine. For example, an emphasis on doctrine can produce an empty, dead, perfunctory orthodoxy. We all have known people who have fat heads and skinny hearts. They are brainiacs without love. It is easy enough to have heads full of information but little transformation. J. C. Ryle stated, "Sound Protestant and evangelical doctrine is useless if it is not accompanied by a holy life."[b] The fact that cold hearts for God can exist in a body with a full head of doctrine should not lead us to avoid doctrine.

But doctrine is not useless. The famous preacher Charles Haddon Spurgeon declared to his church that the value of this confession is that it makes you fit for controversy, faith, edification, and righteousness. It is the place where the younger members of the church will find a compass. He says:

> This little volume is not issued as an authoritative rule, or code of faith, whereby you are to be fettered, but as an assistance to you in controversy, a confirmation in faith, and a means of edification in righteousness. Here the younger members of our church will have a body of divinity in small compass, and by means of the scriptural proofs, will be ready

to give a reason for the hope that is in them.
Be not ashamed of your faith; remember it is the ancient
Gospel of martyrs, confessors, reformers, and saints. Above
all, it is the Truth of God against which the gates of hell
cannot prevail. Let your lives adorn your faith, let your
example recommend your creed. Above all, live in Christ
Jesus, and walk in Him, giving credence to no teaching but
that which is manifestly approved of Him, and owned by the
Holy Spirit. Cleave fast to the Word of God, which is here
mapped out to you.[c]

The Worst and Best of Times

The worst times in history are always characterized by one thing, everyone does "what is right in his own eyes" (Judg. 21:25). In contrast, the best times in history are characterized by "people who know their God" and therefore are "strong, and carry out great exploits" (Dan. 11:32). The difference is in knowing God – truly knowing Him. And you cannot know Him without knowing about Him. That is what this confession can help you to do.

This confession is a treasure chest of the doctrines of the Christian faith. It was written for families. It was written for churches. It keeps you from fads. It protects you from being "tossed...about with every wind of doctrine" (Eph. 4:14). It helps you to guard what has been committed to you (1 Tim. 6:20). It is personal training in the whole counsel of God. It is a guide for family instruction. It is a preserver of church unity. It is a training tool for young people. It is a standard for quelling controversy in the church. I commend it to you for the acquisition of treasure and the adoration of God and the happiness they bring.

LETTER TO THE
— READER —

Courteous Reader,

It is now many years since many of us (with other sober Christians then living and walking in the way of the Lord that we profess) did conceive ourselves to be under a necessity of publishing a confession of our faith. This publication was for the information and satisfaction of those that did not throughly understand what our principles were or had entertained prejudices against our profession. For some men of note by reason of the strange representation of them had taken very wrong measures and accordingly led others into misapprehensions of us and them. And this was first put forth about the year 1643.

The Testimony of Seven Congregations

In the name of seven congregations then gathered in London, since which time, diverse impressions thereof have been dispersed abroad and our end proposed. These have been in good measure answered inasmuch as many (and some of those men eminent both for piety and learning) were thereby satisfied, that we were no way guilty of those heterodoxies and fundamental errors, which had too frequently been charged upon us without ground or occasion given on our part. And forasmuch as that confession is not now commonly to be had and also that many others have since embraced the same truth which is owned therein, it was judged necessary by us to join together in giving a testimony to the world of our firm adhering to those wholesome principles. We have therefore published that which is now in your hand.

The Reasons for Writing the Confession

And forasmuch as our method and manner of expressing our sentiments in this does vary from the former (although the substance of the matter is the same), we shall freely impart to you the reason and occasion thereof. One thing that greatly prevailed with us to undertake this work was not only to give a full account of ourselves to those Christians that differ from us about the subject of baptism, but also to give the profit that might from thence arise unto those that have any account of our labors. This profit would be in their instruction and establishment in the great truths of the Gospel, in the clear understanding and steady belief of which our comfortable walking with God and fruitfulness before Him in all our ways is most nearly concerned. Therefore we did conclude it necessary to express ourselves the more fully and distinctly. We also thought it necessary to fix on such a method as might be most comprehensive of those things which we designed to explain our sense and belief of. Finding no defect, in this regard in that fixed on by the assembly and after them by those of the congregational way, we did readily conclude it best to retain the same order in our present confession. Also when we observed that those last mentioned did in their confession (for reasons which seemed of weight both to themselves and others) choose not only to express their mind in words concurrent with the former in sense concerning all those articles wherein they were agreed but also for the most part without any variation of the terms, we did in like manner conclude it best to follow their example in making use of the very same words with them. This we did both in these articles (which are very many) wherein our faith and doctrine is the same with theirs. And this we did the more abundantly to manifest our consent with both in all the fundamental articles of the Christian religion, as also with many others whose orthodox confessions have been published to the world on behalf of the Protestants in many nations and cities. Also we did this to convince all that we have no itch to clog religion with new words, but do readily acquiesce in that form of sound words, which has been in consent with the Holy Scriptures used by others before us. We hereby declare before God, angels, & men our hearty agreement with them, in that wholesome Protestant doctrine, which with so clear evidence of Scriptures they have asserted. Some things indeed are in some places added, some terms omitted, and some few changed. But these alterations are of that nature as that we need not doubt any charge or suspicion of unsoundness in the faith from any of our brethren upon the account of them.

Desire for Humility and Modesty

In those things wherein we differ from others, we have expressed ourselves with all candor and plainness. This we did that none might entertain jealousy of ought secretly lodged in our breasts that we would not the world should be acquainted with. Yet we hope we have also observed those rules of modesty and humility as will render our freedom, in this respect, inoffensive even to those whose sentiments are different from ours.

To Promote Noble Bereans

We have also taken care to affix texts of Scripture in the margin for the confirmation of each article in our confession. In this work, we have studiously endeavored to select such as are most clear and pertinent for the proof of what is asserted by us. And our earnest desire is that all into whose hands this may come would follow that never-enough-commended example of the noble Bereans. These searched the Scriptures daily that they might find out whether the things preached to them were so or not.

Not for Contention

There is one thing more which we sincerely profess and earnestly desire credence in. Contention is most remote from our design in all that we have done in this matter. We hope the liberty of an ingenuous unfolding of our principles and opening our hearts unto our brethren with the Scripture grounds on which our faith and practice leans will by none of them be either denied to us or taken ill from us.

Our whole design is accomplished if we may obtain that justice as to be measured in our principles and practice and the judgment of both by others, according to what we have now published. The Lord (whose eyes are as a flame of fire) knows to be the doctrine which with our hearts we must firmly believe and sincerely endeavor to conform our lives to. And oh that other contentions being laid asleep, the only care and contention of all, upon whom the name of our blessed Redeemer is called, might for the future be to walk humbly with their God and, in the exercise of all love and meekness towards each other, to perfect holiness in the fear of the Lord. May each one endeavor to have his conversation such as becomes the Gospel. Let them also have their conversation, suitable to his place and capacity, vigorously to promote in others the practice of true religion and undefiled in the sight of God and our Father.

Reforming Our Own Hearts

And that in this backsliding day, we desire that we might not spend our breath in fruitless complaints of the evils of others. Instead may everyone begin at home to reform in the first place our own hearts and ways and then to quicken all that we may have influence upon to the same work. For if the will of God were so, none might deceive themselves by resting in and trusting to a form of godliness without the power of it and inward experience of the efficacy of those truths that are professed by them.

The Cause of Decay Identified – Neglect of Worship in Families

And verily there is one spring and cause of the decay of religion in our day, which we cannot but touch upon and earnestly urge a redress of. This is the neglect of the worship of God in families, by those to whom the charge and conduct of them is committed. May not the gross ignorance and instability of many with the profaneness of others be justly charged upon their parents and masters? For they have not trained them up in the way wherein they ought to walk when they were young. Instead, they have neglected those frequent and solemn commands which the Lord has laid upon them so to catechize and instruct them. For in so doing, their tender years might be seasoned with the knowledge of the truth of God as revealed in the Scriptures. Also they have made an omission of prayer and other duties of religion in their families. They have given an ill example by their loose conversation, and have inured them first to a neglect and then contempt of all piety and religion. We know this will not excuse the blindness or wickedness of any. But certainly it will fall heavy upon those that have thus been the occasion thereof. They indeed die in their sins. However, will not their blood be required of those under whose care they were, who yet permitted them to go on without warning, yea led them into the paths of destruction? And will not the diligence of Christians with respect to the discharge of these duties in ages past rise up in judgment against and condemn many of those who would be esteemed such now?

Our Prayer

We shall conclude with our earnest prayer that the God of all grace will pour out those measures of His Holy Spirit upon us. May God grant that the profession of truth may be accompanied with the sound belief and diligent practice of it by us and that His name may in all things be glorified through Jesus Christ our Lord. Amen.

THE SECOND LONDON BAPTIST CONFESSION

OF 1689

Chapter 1

Of the Holy Scriptures

Pray to God to take off the vail on the Scriptures, that you may understand it; and the vail on your heart, that you may believe it. Pray that God will not only give you his word as a rule of holiness, but his grace as a principle of holiness. Implore the guidance of God's Spirit. Neh. ix. 20: "Thou gavest them thy good Spirit to instruct them." Though the ship hath a compass to sail by, and the store of tackling, yet without a gale of wind it cannot sail; though we have the word written as our compass to sail by, and make use of our endeavors as the tackling, yet unless the Spirit of God blow upon us, we cannot sail with profit.[d]
– Thomas Watson

Chapter 1

ARTICLE I

The Holy
Scripture
is the only
sufficient,
certain, and
infallible rule
of all saving
knowledge,
faith, and
obedience...

The Holy Scripture is the only sufficient, certain, and infallible rule of all saving knowledge, faith, and obedience;[1] although the light of nature and the works of creation and providence do so far manifest the goodness, wisdom, and power of God, as to leave men inexcusable;[2] yet are they not sufficient to give that knowledge of God and His will, which is necessary unto salvation.[3] Therefore it pleased the Lord at sundry times and in divers manners to reveal Himself and to declare that His will unto His Church;[4] and afterward for the better preserving and propagating of the truth, and for the more sure establishment and comfort of the Church against the corruption of the flesh and the malice of Satan and of the world, to commit the same wholly unto writing; which makes the Holy Scriptures to be most necessary,[5] those former ways of God's revealing His will unto His people being now ceased.[6]

[1] Isa. 8:20; Luke 16:29, 31; Eph. 2:20; 2 Tim. 3:15-17

[2] Ps. 19:1-3; Rom. 1:19-21, 32; 2:12a, 14-15

[3] Ps. 19:1-3 with vv. 7-11; Rom. 1:19-21; 2:12a, 14-15 with 1:16-17; and 3:21

[4] Heb. 1:1-2a

[5] Deut. 17:18ff.; 31:9ff., 19ff.; Pro. 22:19-21; Luke 1:1-4; Rom. 1:8-15; 15:4; 1 Cor. 15:1; Gal. 4:20; 6:11; 2 Thess. 2:1-2, 15; 3:17; 1 Tim. 3:14ff.; 2 Pet. 1:12-15, 19-21; 3:1; Rev. 1:9, 19; 2:1, etc.

[6] Acts 1:21-22; 1 Cor. 9:1; 15:7-8; Eph. 2:20; Heb. 1:1-2a

ARTICLE 2

Under the name of Holy Scripture or the Word of God written are now contained all the books of the Old and New Testament which are these:

OF THE OLD TESTAMENT

Genesis, Exodus, Leviticus, Numbers, Deuteronomy, Joshua, Judges, Ruth, 1 Samuel, 2 Samuel, 1 Kings, 2 Kings, 1 Chronicles, 2 Chronicles, Ezra, Nehemiah, Esther, Job, Psalms, Proverbs, Ecclesiastes, The Song of Solomon, Isaiah, Jeremiah, Lamentations, Ezekiel, Daniel, Hosea, Joel, Amos, Obadiah, Jonah, Micah, Nahum, Habakkuk, Zephaniah, Haggai, Zechariah, Malachi.

OF THE NEW TESTAMENT

Matthew, Mark, Luke, John, the Acts of the Apostles, Paul's Epistle to the Romans, 1 Corinthians, 2 Corinthians, Galatians, Ephesians, Philippians, Colossians, 1 Thessalonians, 2 Thessalonians, 1 Timothy, 2 Timothy, Titus, Philemon, the epistle to the Hebrews, the epistle of James, the first and second epistles of Peter, the first, second, and third epistles of John, the epistle of Jude, the Revelation.

All which are given by the inspiration of God to be the rule of faith and life.[7]

[7] 2 Tim. 3:16 with 1 Tim. 5:17-18; 2 Pet. 3:16

All which are given by the inspiration of God to be the rule of faith and life.

Chapter 1

ARTICLE 3

The books commonly called Apocrypha, not being of Divine inspiration, are no part of the canon (or rule) of the Scripture, and therefore are of no authority to the Church of God, nor to be any otherwise approved or made use of than other human writings.[8]

[8] Luke 24:27, 44; Rom. 3:2

ARTICLE 4

The authority of the Holy Scripture, for which it ought to be believed, depends not upon the testimony of any man or church;[9] but wholly upon God (who is truth itself) the Author thereof; therefore it is to be received because it is the Word of God.[10]

[9] Luke 16:27-31; Gal. 1:8-9; Eph. 2:20
[10] Matt. 4:1-11; 5:17-18; 13:35; 22:32; 22:41ff.; 26:54; Luke 16:17; 22:37; John 10:35; 13:18; 19:34-36; 19:24; Acts 1:16; 2:16, 24ff.; 4:25; 13:34-35; Rom. 1:2; 3:2; 9:17; 15:4; 1 Cor. 10:11; Gal. 3:8, 16; 2 Thess. 2:13; 2 Tim. 3:15-16; 2 Pet. 1:19-21; 1 John 5:9

The authority of the Holy Scripture... depends... wholly upon God (who is truth itself) the Author thereof...

ARTICLE 5

We may be moved and induced by the testimony of the Church of God to a high and reverent esteem of the Holy Scriptures;[11] and the heavenliness of the matter, the efficacy of the doctrine, and the majesty of the style, the consent of all the parts, the scope of the whole (which is to give all glory to God), the full discovery it makes of the only way of man's salvation, and many other incomparable excellencies, and entire perfections thereof are arguments whereby it does abundantly evidence itself to be the Word of God;[12] yet notwithstanding, our full persuasion and assurance of the infallible truth and Divine authority thereof is from the inward work of the Holy Spirit bearing witness by and with the Word in our hearts.[13]

[11] 2 Tim. 3:14-15
[12] Deut. 31:11-13; Jer. 23:28-29; Mark 16:15-16; Luke 16:27-31; John 6:63; 20:31; Gal. 1:8-9; Heb. 4:12-13; 1 Pet. 1:23-25
[13] Matt. 16:17; John 3:3; 16:13-14; 1 Cor. 2:4-5, 10-12, 14ff.; 1 Thess. 1:5-6; 1 John 2:20-21 with v.27

ARTICLE 6

The whole counsel of God concerning all things necessary for His own glory, man's salvation, faith, and life is either expressly set down or necessarily contained in the Holy Scripture, unto which nothing at any time is to be added, whether by new revelation of the Spirit or traditions of men.[14]

Nevertheless we acknowledge the inward illumination of the Spirit of God to be necessary for the saving understanding of such things as are revealed in the Word,[15] and that there are some circumstances concerning the worship of God and government of the Church common to human actions and societies, which are to be ordered by the light of nature and Christian prudence according to the general rules of the Word, which are always to be observed.[16]

...is either expressly set down or necessarily contained in the Holy Scripture...

[14] Deut. 4:2; Ps. 19:7; 119:6, 9, 104, 128; Acts 20:20, 27;
Gal. 1:8-9; 2 Tim. 3:15-17
[15] John 6:45; 1 Cor. 2:9-14
[16] 1 Cor. 11:13-14; 14:26, 40

ARTICLE 7

All things in Scripture are not alike plain in themselves[17]
nor alike clear unto all,[18] yet those things which are
necessary to be known, believed, and observed for
salvation are so clearly propounded and opened in some
place of Scripture or other that not only the learned but
the unlearned, in a due use of ordinary means, may attain
to a sufficient understanding of them.[19]

[17] 2 Pet. 3:16
[18] 2 Tim. 3:15-17
[19] Deut. 30:11-14; Ps. 19:7-8; 119:105, 130; Pro. 6:22-23; 2
Tim. 3:14-17; 2 Pet. 1:19

ARTICLE 8

The Old Testament in Hebrew (which was the native
language of the people of God of old)[20] and the New
Testament in Greek (which at the time of the writing
of it was most generally known to the nations), being
immediately inspired by God and by His singular care
and providence kept pure in all ages, are therefore
authentic;[21] so as in all controversies of religion the
Church is finally to appeal unto them.[22] But because
these original tongues are not known to all the people of
God, who have a right unto and interest in the Scriptures
and are commanded in the fear of God to read[23] and
search them,[24] therefore they are to be translated into the
vulgar language of every nation, unto which they come,[25]

that the Word of God dwelling plentifully in all, they may worship Him in an acceptable manner and through patience and comfort of the Scriptures may have hope.[26]

[20] Rom. 3:2
[21] Matt. 5:18
[22] Isa. 8:20; John 10:34-36; Acts 15:15; 2 Tim. 3:16-17
[23] Acts 15:15
[24] Deut. 17:18-20; Pro. 2:1-5; 8:34; John 5:39, 46
[25] 1 Cor. 14:6, 9. 11-12, 24, 28
[26] Rom. 15:4; Col. 3:16

ARTICLE 9

The infallible rule of interpretation of Scripture is the Scripture itself, and therefore when there is a question about the true and full sense of any Scripture (which is not manifold but one), it must be searched by other places that speak more clearly.[27]

The infallible rule of interpretation of Scripture is the Scripture itself...

[27] Isa. 8:20; John 10:34-36; Acts 15:15-16 ; 2 Pet. 1:20-21

ARTICLE 10

The supreme judge by which all controversies of religion are to be determined and all decrees of counsels, opinions of ancient writers, doctrines of men, and private spirits are to be examined and in whose sentence we are to rest can be no other but the Holy Scripture delivered by the Spirit, into which Scripture so delivered, our faith is finally resolved.[28]

[28] Matt. 22:29, 31-32; Acts 28:23-25; Eph. 2:20

Chapter 2

Of God and the Holy Trinity

*The highest science, the loftiest speculation, the mightiest philosophy,
which can ever engage the attention of a child of God, is the name, the
nature, the Person, the work, the doings, and the existence of the great
God whom he calls his Father.*[e]
– *C .H. Spurgeon*

Chapter 2

ARTICLE I

The Lord our God is but one only living and true God;[1] whose subsistence is in and of Himself;[2] infinite in being and perfection;[3] whose essence cannot be comprehended by any but Himself;[4] a most pure spirit; invisible; without body, parts, or passions; who only has immortality; dwelling in the light, which no man can approach unto;[5] who is immutable;[6] immense;[7] eternal;[8] incomprehensible; almighty;[9] every way infinite; most holy;[10] most wise; most free; most absolute;[11] working all things according to the counsel of His own immutable and most righteous will,[12] for His own glory;[13] most loving, gracious, merciful, longsuffering; abundant in goodness and truth; forgiving iniquity, transgression, and sin;[14] the rewarder of them that diligently seek Him; and withal most just and terrible in His judgments, hating all sin; and who will by no means clear the guilty.[15]

The Lord our God is... most holy;... terrible in His judgments, hating all sin; and who will by no means clear the guilty.

[1] Deut. 6:4; Jer. 10:10; 1 Cor. 8:4, 6; 1 Thess. 1:9
[2] Isa. 48:12; Jer. 10:10
[3] Isa. 48:12
[4] Exo. 3:14; Job 11:7-8; 26:14; Ps. 145:3; Rom. 11:33-34
[5] Deut. 4:15-16; Luke 24:39; John 4:24; Acts 14:11, 15; 1 Tim. 1:17; Jas. 5:17
[6] Mal. 3:6
[7] 1 Kgs. 8:27; Jer. 23:23
[8] Ps. 90:2
[9] Gen. 17:1
[10] Isa. 6:3
[11] Gen. 17:1; Exo. 3:14; 1 Kgs. 8:27; Ps. 90:2; 115:3; Isa. 6:3; Jer. 23:23-24; Mal. 3:6; Rom. 16:27; 1 Tim. 1:17; Jas. 1:17; Rev. 4:8
[12] Ps. 115:3; Isa. 46:10
[13] Isa. 46:10; Pro. 16:4; Rom. 11:36; Eph. 1:11

[14] Exo. 34:6-7; 1 John 4:8
[15] Exo. 34:6-7; Neh. 9:32-33; Ps. 5:5-6; Nah. 1:2-3; Heb. 11:6

ARTICLE 2

God having all life, glory, goodness, blessedness in and of Himself is alone in and unto Himself all sufficient, not standing in need of any creature which He has made, nor deriving any glory from them, but only manifesting His own glory in, by, unto, and upon them,[16] He is the alone fountain of all being, of whom, through whom, and to whom are all things, and He has most sovereign dominion over all creatures to do by them, for them, or upon them, whatsoever Himself pleases;[17] in His sight all things are open and manifest, His knowledge is infinite, infallible, and independent upon the creature, so as nothing is to Him contingent or uncertain;[18] He is most holy in all His counsels, in all His works, and in all His commands;[19] to Him is due from angels and men whatsoever worship, service, or obedience as creatures they owe unto the Creator, and whatever He is further pleased to require of them.[20]

[God] has most sovereign dominion over all creatures, to do by them, for them, or upon them, whatsoever Himself pleases.

[16] Job 22:2-3; Ps. 148:13; 119:68; John 5:26; Acts 7:2; 17:24-25;1 Tim. 6:15
[17] Dan. 4:25, 34-35; Rom. 11:34-36; 1 Tim. 6:15; Rev. 4:11
[18] Ps. 147:5; Ezek. 11:5; Acts 15:18; Rom. 11:33-34; Heb. 4:13
[19] Ps. 145:17; Rom. 7:12
[20] Rev. 5:12-14

Chapter 2

ARTICLE 3

...there
are three
subsistences:
the Father,
the Word
(or Son),
and Holy
Spirit – of one
substance,
power, and
eternity; each
having the
whole Divine
essence...

In this Divine and infinite Being, there are three subsistences: the Father, the Word (or Son), and Holy Spirit[21] – of one substance, power, and eternity; each having the whole Divine essence, yet the essence undivided;[22] the Father is of none, neither begotten nor proceeding; the Son is eternally begotten of the Father; the Holy Spirit proceeding from the Father and the Son;[23] all infinite, without beginning, therefore but one God, who is not to be divided in nature and being, but distinguished by several peculiar, relative properties and personal relations; which doctrine of the Trinity is the foundation of all our communion with God and comfortable dependence on Him.

[21] 1 John 5:7; Matt. 3:16-17; 28:19; 2 Cor. 13:14
[22] Exo. 3:14; John 14:11; 1 Cor. 8:6
[23] Pro. 8:22-31; John 1:1-3, 14, 18; 3:16; 10:36; 15:26; 16:28; Gal. 4:4-6; Heb. 1:2; 1 John 4:14

Chapter 3

Of God's Decree

There is no attribute of God more comforting to his children than the doctrine of Divine Sovereignty. Under the most adverse circumstances, in the most severe troubles, they believe that Sovereignty hath ordained their afflictions, that Sovereignty overrules them, and that Sovereignty will sanctify them all. There is nothing for which the children of God ought more earnestly to contend than the dominion of their Master over all creation—the kingship of God over all the works of his own hands—the throne of God, and his right to sit upon that throne.[f]
– C. H. Spurgeon

Chapter 3

ARTICLE 1

God has decreed in Himself from all eternity, by the most wise and holy counsel of His own will...

God has decreed in Himself from all eternity, by the most wise and holy counsel of His own will, freely and unchangeably,[1] all things whatsoever comes to pass;[2] yet so as thereby is God neither the author of sin nor has fellowship with any therein[3] nor is violence offered to the will of the creature nor yet is the liberty or contingency of second causes taken away but rather established,[4] in which appears His wisdom in disposing all things, and power and faithfulness in accomplishing His decree.[5]

[1] Ps. 115:3; 135:6; Pro. 19:21; Isa. 14:24-27; 46:10-11; Rom. 9:19
[2] Isa. 46:10; Dan. 4:34-35; Rom. 8:28; 9:15, 18; 11:36; Eph. 1:11; Heb. 6:17
[3] Gen. 18:25; Jas. 1:13, 15, 17; 1 John 1:5
[4] Gen. 50:20; 2 Sam. 24:1; Isa. 10:5-7; Matt. 17:12; John 19:11; Acts 2:23; 4:27-28
[5] Num. 23:19; Eph. 1:3-5

ARTICLE 2

Although God knows whatsoever may or can come to pass upon all supposed conditions,[6] yet has He not decreed anything because He foresaw it as future or as that which would come to pass upon such conditions.[7]

[6] 1 Sam 23:11-12; Matt. 11:21, 23; Acts 15:18
[7] Isa. 40:13-14; Rom. 9:11-18; 11:34; 1 Cor. 2:16

ARTICLE 3

By the decree of God for the manifestation of His glory, some men and angels are predestinated or foreordained to eternal life, through Jesus Christ[8] to the praise of His glorious grace;[9] others being left to act in their sin to their just condemnation to the praise of His glorious justice.[10]

[8] Matt. 25:34, 41; 1 Tim. 5:21
[9] Matt. 25:34; Eph. 1:5-6; 1 Tim. 5:21
[10] Rom. 9:22-23; Jude 4

ARTICLE 4

These angels and men thus predestinated and foreordained are particularly and unchangeably designed, and their number so certain and definite that it cannot be either increased or diminished.[11]

[11] Matt. 22:1-14; John 13:18; Rom. 11:5-6; 1 Cor. 7:20-22; 2 Tim. 2:19

ARTICLE 5

Those of mankind that are predestinated to life, God before the foundation of the world was laid, according to His eternal and immutable purpose and the secret counsel and good pleasure of His will, has chosen in Christ unto everlasting glory, out of His mere free grace and love,[12] without any other thing in the creature as a condition or cause moving Him thereunto.[13]

...according to His eternal and immutable purpose and the secret counsel and good pleasure of His will...

[12] Rom. 8:30; Eph. 1:4-6, 9, 11; 1 Thess. 5:9; 2 Tim. 1:9
[13] Rom. 9:11-16; 11:5-6; Eph. 2:5, 12

ARTICLE 6

As God has appointed the elect unto glory, so He has by the eternal and most free purpose of His will, foreordained all the means thereunto;[14] wherefore they

who are elected, being fallen in Adam, are redeemed by
Christ;[15] are effectually called unto faith in Christ by
His Spirit working in due season; are justified, adopted,
sanctified,[16] and kept by His power through faith unto
salvation;[17] neither are any other redeemed by Christ
or effectually called, justified, adopted, sanctified, and
saved, but the elect only.[18]

[14] Eph. 1:4; 2:10; 2 Thess. 2:13; 1 Pet. 1:2
[15] 1 Thess. 5:9-10; Tit. 2:14
[16] Rom. 8:30; Eph. 1:5; 2 Thess. 2:13
[17] 1 Pet. 1:5
[18] John 6:64-65; 8:47; 10:26; 17:9; Rom. 8:28; 1 John 2:19

ARTICLE 7

The doctrine of this high mystery of predestination is
to be handled with special prudence and care,[19] that
men attending the will of God revealed in His Word and
yielding obedience thereunto may, from the certainty
of their effectual vocation, be assured of their eternal
election;[20] so shall this doctrine afford matter of praise,
reverence, and admiration of God,[21] and of humility,[22]
diligence,[23] and abundant consolation to all that sincerely
obey the Gospel.[24]

...so shall
this doctrine
afford matter
of praise...

[19] Deut. 29:29; Rom. 9:20; 11:33
[20] 1 Thess. 1:4-5; 2 Pet. 1:10
[21] Rom. 11:33; Eph. 1:6
[22] Rom. 11:5-6, 20; Col. 3:12
[23] 2 Pet. 1:10
[24] Luke 10:20

Chapter 4

Of Creation

*God has made everything for man's service; the corn for nourishment,
the beasts for usefulness, the birds for music, that man should be for
God's service. The rivers come from the sea, and they run into the sea
again. All we have is from God. Let us honour our Creator, and
live to him that made us.*[g]
– Thomas Watson

Chapter 4

ARTICLE 1

In the beginning, it pleased God the Father, Son, and Holy Spirit[1] for the manifestation of the glory of His eternal power, wisdom, and goodness[2] to create or make the world and all things therein, whether visible or invisible,[3] in the space of six days[4] and all very good.[5]

[1] Gen. 1:2; Job 26:13; 33:4; John 1:2-3; Heb. 1:2
[2] Ps. 104:24; 33:5-6; Pro. 3:19; Jer. 10:12; Acts 14:15-16; Rom. 1:20
[3] Gen. 1:1; John 1:2; Col. 1:16
[4] Gen. 2:1-3; Exo. 20:8-11
[5] Gen. 1:31; 2:1-2; Eccl. 7:29; Rom. 5:12; Col. 1:16

ARTICLE 2

After God had made all other creatures, He created man, male and female, with reasonable and immortal souls, rendering them fit unto that life to God for which they were created;[6] being made after the image of God, in knowledge, righteousness, and true holiness;[7] having the Law of God written in their hearts,[8] and power to fulfill it; and yet under a possibility of transgressing, being left to the liberty of their own will, which was subject to change.[9]

[6] Gen. 1:27; 2:7; Eccl. 12:7; Matt. 10:28; Jas. 2:26
[7] Gen. 1:26-27; 5:1-3; 9:6; Eccl. 7:29; 1 Cor. 11:7; Jas. 3:9; Eph. 4:24; Col. 3:10
[8] Rom. 2:14-15
[9] Gen. 3:6; Eccl. 7:29; Rom. 1:14-15, 32; 2:12a; 5:12

ARTICLE 3

Besides the Law written in their hearts, they received a command not to eat of the tree of knowledge of good and evil, which whilst they kept, they were happy in their communion with God and had dominion over the creatures.[10]

[10] Gen. 1:26, 28; 2:17

Chapter 5

Of Divine Providence

*Learn quietly to submit to divine providence. Do not murmur at things
that are ordered by divine wisdom. We may no more find fault with the
works of providence than we may with the works of creation. It is a sin
as much to quarrel with God's providence as to deny his providence.
If men do not act as we would have them, they shall act as God would
have them. His providence is his master-wheel that turns these lesser
wheels, and God will bring his glory out of all at last. 'I was dumb and
opened not my mouth, because thou didst it.' Psa xxxix 9.*[h]
– Thomas Watson

Chapter 5

God, the good
Creator of all
things...

ARTICLE 1

God, the good Creator of all things,[1] in His infinite power
and wisdom,[2] does uphold, direct, dispose, and govern[3]
all creatures and things,[4] from the greatest even to the
least,[5] by His most wise and holy providence,[6] to the
end for the which they were created,[7] according unto
His infallible foreknowledge and the free and immutable
counsel of His own will,[8] to the praise of the glory of His
wisdom, power, justice, infinite goodness, and mercy.[9]

[1] Gen. 1:31; 2:18; Ps. 119:68
[2] Ps. 66:7; 145:11; Pro. 3:19
[3] Job 38-41; Ps. 135:6; Isa. 46:10-11; Dan. 4:34-35; Acts
17:25-28; Heb. 1:3
[4] Job 38:11; Ps. 135:6; Isa. 46:10-11; Heb. 1:3
[5] Matt. 10:29-31
[6] Ps. 104:24; 145:17; Pro. 15:3
[7] Col. 1:16-17; Acts 17:24-28
[8] Ps. 33:10-11; Eph. 1:11
[9] Gen. 45:7; Ps. 145:7; Isa. 63:14; Rom. 9:17; Eph. 1:11;
3:10

ARTICLE 2

Although in relation to the foreknowledge and decree of
God, the first cause, all things come to pass immutably
and infallibly so that there is not anything [that] befalls
any by chance or without His providence;[10] yet by the
same providence, He orders them to fall out, according
to the nature of second causes either necessarily, freely,
or contingently.[11]

[10] Pro. 16:33; Acts 2:23
[11] Gen. 8:22; Exo. 21:13; Deut. 19:5; Ruth 2:3;

1 Kgs. 22:28, 34; Pro. 20:18; 21:31; Isa. 10:6-7; Jer. 31:35; Matt. 5:20-21; Luke 13:3, 5; 14:25ff.; Acts 27:31; Phil. 1:19

ARTICLE 3

God in His ordinary providence makes use of means;[12] yet is free to work without,[13] above,[14] and against them[15] at His pleasure.

[12] Isa. 55:10-11; Hos. 2:21-22; Acts 27:22, 31, 44
[13] Hos. 1:7; Luke 1:34-35
[14] Rom. 4:19-21
[15] Exo. 3:2-3; 2 Kgs. 6:6; Dan. 3:27

ARTICLE 4

The almighty power, unsearchable wisdom, and infinite goodness of God so far manifest themselves in His providence that His determinate counsel extends itself even to the first Fall and all other sinful actions both of angels and men;[16] (and that not by a bare permission) which also He most wisely and powerfully bounds and otherwise orders and governs in a manifold dispensation to His most holy ends;[17] yet so as the sinfulness of their acts proceeds only from the creatures and not from God, who being most holy and righteous, neither is nor can be the author or approver of sin.[18]

[God] being most holy and righteous, neither is nor can be the author or approver of sin.

[16] 2 Sam. 24:1; 1 Chr. 21:1; Rom. 11:32-34
[17] Gen. 50:20; 2 Kgs. 19:28; Ps. 76:10; Isa. 10: 6-7,12; Acts 14:16
[18] Ps. 50:21; Jas. 1:13, 14, 17; 1 John 2:16

ARTICLE 5

The most wise, righteous, and gracious God does oftentimes leave for a season His own children to manifold temptations and the corruptions of their own heart to chastise them for their former sins or to discover unto them the hidden strength of corruption and deceitfulness of their hearts that they may be humbled and to raise them to a more close and constant dependence for their support upon Himself and to make them more watchful against all future occasions of sin and for other just and holy ends.[19] So that whatsoever befalls any of His elect is by His appointment, for His glory, and their good.[20]

[19] 2 Sam. 24:1; 2 Chr. 32:25-26, 31; Mark 14:66f.; Luke 2:34-35; John 21:15-17; 2 Cor. 12:7-9
[20] Rom. 8:28

ARTICLE 6

As for those wicked and ungodly men, whom God as a righteous judge, for former sin, does blind and harden;[21] from them He not only withholds His grace, whereby they might have been enlightened in their understanding and wrought upon in their hearts;[22] but sometimes also withdraws the gifts which they had[23] and exposes them to such objects as their corruptions makes occasion of sin;[24] and withal gives them over to their own lusts, the temptations of the world, and the power of Satan[25] whereby it comes to pass that they harden themselves even under those means which God uses for the softening of others.[26]

[21] Rom. 1:24-26, 28; 11:7-8
[22] Deut. 29:4
[23] Matt. 13:12; 25:29
[24] Deut. 2:30; 2 Kgs. 8:12-13
[25] Ps. 81:11-12; 2 Thess. 2:10-12
[26] Exo. 7:3; 8:15, 32; Isa. 6:9-10; 8:14; John 12:39-40; Acts 28:26-27; 2 Cor. 2:15-16; 1 Pet. 2:7-8

ARTICLE 7

As the providence of God does in general reach to all creatures; so after a most special manner, it takes care of His Church and disposes of all things to the good thereof.[27]

[27] Pro. 2:7-8; Isa. 43:3-5, 14; Amos 9:8-9; Rom. 8:28; Eph. 1:11, 22; 3:10-11, 21; 1 Tim. 4:10

Of the Fall of Man, of Sin, and of the Punishment Thereof

Sin aims always at the utmost; every time it rises up to tempt or entice, might it have its own course, it would go out to the utmost sin in that kind. Every unclean thought or glance would be adultery if it could; every covetous desire would be oppression, every thought of unbelief would be atheism, might it grow to its head. Men may come to that, that sin may not be heard speaking a scandalous word in their hearts—that is, provoking to any great sin with scandal in its mouth; but yet every rise of lust, might it have its course, would come to the height of villainy: it is like the grave, that is never satisfied. And herein lies no small share of the deceitfulness of sin, by which it prevails to the hardening of men, and so to their ruin (Heb. 3:13).[i]
– John Owen

Chapter 6

ARTICLE 1

Although God created man upright and perfect and
gave him a righteous law, which had been unto life
had he kept it, and threatened death upon the breach
thereof, yet he did not long abide in this honor;[1] Satan
using the subtlety of the serpent to seduce Eve, then
by her seducing Adam, who without any compulsion
did willfully transgress the law of their creation and the
command given unto them in eating the forbidden fruit;[2]
which God was pleased according to His wise and holy
counsel to permit, having purposed to order it to His
own glory.[3]

[1] Gen. 2:16-17; 4:25-5:3; Eccl. 7:29; Rom. 5:12a, 14-15
[2] Gen. 3:1-7, 12-13; 2 Cor. 11:3; 1 Tim. 2:14
[3] 2 Sam. 16:10; 24:1; 1 Kgs. 22:22-23; 1 Chr. 21:1; Acts
2:23; 4:27-28; Rom. 11:32-34

ARTICLE 2

Our first parents, by this sin, fell from their original
righteousness and communion with God and we in
them, whereby death came upon all;[4] all becoming dead
in sin[5] and wholly defiled in all the faculties and parts of
soul and body.[6]

Our first
parents...
fell from
their original
righteousness
and
communion
with God, and
we in them...

[4] Gen. 3:22-24; 8:21; Ps. 51:4-5; Pro. 22:15; Rom. 3:23;
5:12ff.; 1 Cor. 15:20-22; 58:3; Eph. 2:1-3
[5] Rom 5:12-21
[6] Gen. 2:17; 6:5; Jer. 17:9; John 5:40; Rom. 1:21; 3:10-19;
8:7; Eph. 2:1; 4:17-19; Tit. 1:15

ARTICLE 3

They being the root, and, by God's appointment, standing in the room and stead of all mankind, the guilt of the sin was imputed, and corrupted nature conveyed to all their posterity, descending from them by ordinary generation,[7] being now conceived in sin[8] and by nature children of wrath,[9] the servants of sin, the subjects of death[10] and all other miseries (spiritual, temporal, and eternal), unless the Lord Jesus set them free.[11]

They being the root, and, by God's appointment, standing in the room and stead of all mankind...

[7] Rom. 5:12-19; 1 Cor. 15:21-22, 45, 49
[8] Job 14:4; Ps. 51:5
[9] Eph. 2:3
[10] Rom. 5:12; 6:20
[11] Gen. 8:21; Job 14:4; 15:14; Ps. 51:4-5; 58:3; Pro. 22:15; Rom. 5:12ff.; 1 Cor. 15:20-22; Eph. 2:1-3; 1 Thess. 1:10; Heb. 2:14-15

ARTICLE 4

From this original corruption (whereby we are utterly indisposed, disabled, and made opposite to all good and wholly inclined to all evil)[12] do proceed all actual transgressions.[13]

[12] Matt. 7:17-18; 12:33-35; Luke 6:43-45; John 3:3, 5; 6:37, 39, 40, 44-45, 65; Rom. 3:10-12; 5:6; 7:18; 8:7-8; 1 Cor. 2:14; Col. 1:21
[13] Matt. 7:17-20; 12:33-35; 15:18-20; Jas. 1:14-15

ARTICLE 5

The corruption of nature during this life does remain in those that are regenerated;[14] and although it be through

Chapter 6

Christ pardoned and mortified, yet both itself and the first motions thereof are truly and properly sin.[15]

[14] 1 Kgs. 8:46; Ps. 130:3; 143:2; Pro. 20:9; Eccl. 7:20; Rom. 7:14-25; Jas. 3:2; 1 John 1:8-10

[15] Gen. 8:21; Ps. 51:4-5; Pro. 15:26; 21:4; 22:15; Matt. 5:27-28; Rom. 7:5, 7-8, 17-18, 23-25; 8:3-13; Gal. 5:17-24; Eph. 2:3

Chapter 7

Of God's Covenant

But their sins shall not shake my covenant with my Beloved, nor cause that I for ever should reject them. 'My covenant will I not break, nor alter the thing that is gone out of my lips. His seed will I make to endure for ever, his seed shall endure for ever.' (Psa 89:30-36) Hence, it is clear that the covenant stands good to us as long as Christ stands good to God, or before his face; for he is not only our Mediator by covenant, but he himself is our conditions to God-ward. Therefore he is said to be 'a covenant of the people,' or that which the holy God, by law, required of us. (Isa 42:6)[j]
– John Bunyan

Chapter 7

The distance
between
God and the
creature is so
great...

The distance between God and the creature is so great
that although reasonable creatures do owe obedience
unto Him as their Creator, yet they could never have
attained the reward of life but by some voluntary
condescension on God's part, which He has been pleased
to express by way of covenant.[1]

[1] Job 35:7-8; Ps. 113:5-6; Isa. 40:13-16; Luke 17:5-10; Acts
17:24-25

Moreover man having brought himself under the curse
of the Law by his fall, it pleased the Lord to make a
Covenant of Grace,[2] wherein He freely offers unto
sinners, life and salvation by Jesus Christ, requiring of
them faith in Him that they may be saved[3] and promising
to give unto all those that are ordained unto eternal life
His Holy Spirit to make them willing and able to believe.[4]

[2] Gen. 2:17; 3:15; Ps. 110:4 (with Heb. 7:18-22; 10:12-18);
Rom. 3:20-21; Gal. 3:10; Eph. 2:12 (with Rom. 4:13-17 and
Gal. 3:18-22); Heb. 9:15
[3] Mark 16:15-16; John 3:16; Rom. 8:3; 10:6, 9; Gal. 3:11
[4] Ps. 110:3; Ezek. 36:26-27; John 6:44-45

This covenant is revealed in the Gospel, first of all to
Adam in the promise of salvation by the seed of the
woman and afterwards by farther steps, until the full
discovery thereof was completed in the New Testament;[5]
and it is founded in that eternal covenant transaction
that was between the Father and the Son about the

redemption of the elect;[6] and it is alone by the grace of this covenant that all of the posterity of fallen Adam that ever were saved did obtain life and a blessed immortality, man being now utterly incapable of acceptance with God upon those terms on which Adam stood in his state of innocency.[7]

[5] Gen. 3:15; Rom. 16:25-27; Eph. 3:5; Tit. 1:2; Heb. 1:1-2
[6] Ps. 110:4; Eph. 1:3-11; 2 Tim. 1:9; Tit. 1:2
[7] John 8:56; Acts 4:12; Rom. 4:1-25; Heb. 11:6, 13

Chapter 8

Of Christ the Mediator

Christ being a Mediator of Reconciliation and Intercession, implies the infinite Value of his Blood and Sufferings, as that which in itself was sufficient to stop the Course of God's Justice, and render him not only placable, but abundantly satisfied and well pleased, even with those that before were Enemies: And so much is said of it, Col. i.21, 22...Surely, that which can cause the Holy God, justly incensed against Sinners, to lay aside all his Wrath, and take an Enemy into his Bosom, and establish such an Amity as can never more be broken, but to rest in his Love, and joy over him with Singing, as it is, Zeph. iii.17. This must be a most excellent and efficacious Thing.[k]
– John Flavel

ARTICLE 1

It pleased God[1] in His eternal purpose[2] to choose and ordain the Lord Jesus His only begotten Son, according to the covenant made between them both,[3] to be the Mediator between God and Man;[4] the Prophet, Priest, and King; Head and Savior of His Church; the Heir of all things; and Judge of the world;[5] unto whom He did from all eternity give a people to be His seed and to be by Him in time redeemed, called, justified, sanctified, and glorified.[6]

[1] Isa. 42:1; John 3:16
[2] 1 Pet. 1:19
[3] Ps. 110:4; Heb. 7:21-22
[4] Isa. 42:1; 1 Pet. 1:19-20
[5] Ps. 2:6; Luke 1:33; Acts 3:22; 17:31; Eph. 1:22-23; 5:23; 1 Tim. 2:5; Heb. 1:2; 5:5-6
[6] Ps. 22:30; Isa. 53:10; 55:4-5; John 17:6; Rom. 8:30; 1 Cor. 1:30; 1 Tim. 2:6

ARTICLE 2

The Son of God...being very and eternal God, the brightness of the Father's glory, of one substance and equal with Him...

The Son of God (the second Person in the Holy Trinity, being very and eternal God, the brightness of the Father's glory, of one substance and equal with Him; who made the world, who upholds and governs all things He has made[7]) did when the fullness of time was come[8] take unto Him man's nature with all the essential properties[9] and common infirmities thereof,[10] yet without sin;[11] being conceived by the Holy Spirit in the womb of the Virgin Mary, the Holy Spirit coming down upon her and the power of the most High overshadowing her and so was made of a woman, of the tribe of Judah, of the seed of Abraham and David according to the Scriptures;[12]

so that two, whole, perfect, and distinct natures were inseparably joined together in one person, without conversion, composition, or confusion; which person is very God[13] and very man[14] yet one Christ, the only Mediator between God and man.[15]

[7] Ps. 102:25 with Heb. 1:10; Isa. 8:12-13 with 3:15; Joel 2:32 with Rom. 10:13; John 1:1; 5:18; 8:58; 20:28; Rom. 9:5; Tit. 2:13; Phil. 2:5-6; Heb. 1:8-9; 1 Pet. 2:3 with Ps. 34:8; 2 Pet. 1:1; 1 John 5:20

[8] Gal. 4:4

[9] Matt. 4:1-11; 9:10-13, 36; 11:19; 26:12, 26; 26:36-44; Mark 3:5; 10:14; 14:8; Luke 2:40, 52; 5:16; 6:12; 7:44-46; 9:18, 28; 10:21; 19:41-44; 22:44; 23:46; John 11:35; 13:23; 19:30, 32-35; Heb. 2:10; 5:8-9; 10:5; Heb. 4:15 with Jas. 1:13; Jas. 2:26; 1 Pet. 3:18; 4:1

[10] Matt. 4:2; 8:24; 21:18; Mark 11:12; John 1:1-14; 4:6-7; 19:28; Rom. 8:3; Gal. 4:4; Heb. 2:10, 18; 5:8

[11] Isa. 53:9; Luke 1:35; John 8:46; 14:30; Rom. 8:3; 2 Cor. 5:21; Heb. 2:14, 16-17; 4:15; 7:26; 9:14; 1 Pet. 1:19; 2:22; 1 John 3:5

[12] Matt. 1:22-23; Luke 1:27, 31, 35; Rom. 1:3-4; 9:5

[13] See ref. 7 above.

[14] Acts 2:22; 13:38; 17:31; 1 Cor. 15:21; 1 Tim. 2:5

[15] Rom. 1:3-4; 9:5; Gal. 4:4-5; Phil. 2:5-11; 1 Tim. 2:5

ARTICLE 3

The Lord Jesus in His human nature thus united to the Divine in the person of the Son was sanctified and anointed with the Holy Spirit above measure,[16] having in Him all the treasures of wisdom and knowledge, in whom it pleased the Father that all fullness should dwell, to the end that being holy, harmless, undefiled, and full of grace and truth, He might be thoroughly furnished to

...so that two, whole, perfect, and distinct natures were inseparably joined together in one person...

execute the office of a Mediator and surety;[17] which office He took not upon Himself but was thereunto called by His Father;[18] who also put all power and judgment in His hand and gave Him commandment to execute the same.[19]

[16] Ps. 45:7; John 3:34; Acts 10:38
[17] Ps. 45:7; John 1:14; Acts 10:38; Col. 1:19; 2:3; Heb. 7:22, 26
[18] Heb. 5:5
[19] Matt. 28:18; John 5:22, 27; Acts 2:36; Heb. 5:5

ARTICLE 4

This office the Lord Jesus did most willingly undertake,[20] which that He might discharge, He was made under the Law[21] and did perfectly fulfill it and underwent the punishment due to us, which we should have born and suffered,[22] being made sin and a curse for us,[23] enduring most grievous sorrows in His soul and most painful sufferings in His body,[24] was crucified and died and remained in the state of the dead; yet saw no corruption;[25] on the third day, He arose from the dead[26] with the same body in which He suffered;[27] with which He also ascended into heaven[28] and there sits at the right hand of His Father, making intercession,[29] and shall return to judge men and angels at the end of the world.[30]

... on the third day He arose from the dead...

[20] Ps. 40:7-8; John 10:18; Phil. 2:8; Heb. 10:5-10
[21] Matt. 3:15; Gal. 4:4
[22] Isa. 53:6; Matt. 3:15; 5:17; Gal. 3:13; 1 Pet. 3:18
[23] Matt. 26:37-38; 27:46; Luke 22:44; 2 Cor. 5:21
[24] Matt. 26:37-38; 27:46; Matt. 26-27; Luke 22:44
[25] Acts 13:37; Phil. 2:8
[26] 1 Cor. 15:3-4

[27] John 20:25, 27
[28] Mark 16:19; Acts 1:9-11
[29] Rom. 8:34; Heb. 9:24
[30] Matt. 13:40-42; Acts 1:11; 10:42; Rom. 14:9-10;
2 Pet. 2:4; Jude 6

ARTICLE 5

The Lord Jesus by His perfect obedience and sacrifice of Himself,[31] which He through the eternal Spirit once offered up unto God,[32] has fully satisfied the justice of God,[33] procured reconciliation,[34] and purchased an everlasting inheritance in the kingdom of heaven[35] for all those whom the Father has given unto Him.[36]

[31] Rom. 5:19; Eph. 5:2
[32] Heb. 9:14, 16; 10:10, 14
[33] Rom. 3:25-26; Heb. 2:17; 9:14; 10:14; 1 John 2:2; 4:10
[34] 2 Cor 5:18-19; Col. 1:20-23
[35] Heb. 9:15; Rev. 5:9-10
[36] John 17:2; Heb. 9:15

ARTICLE 6

Although the price of redemption was not actually paid by Christ till after His incarnation, yet the virtue, efficacy, and benefit thereof were communicated to the elect in all ages successively from the beginning of the world[37] in and by those promises, types, and sacrifices wherein He was revealed and signified to be the seed of the woman, which should bruise the serpent's head[38] and the Lamb slain from the foundation of the world,[39] being the same yesterday, and today, and forever.[40]

...the Lamb slain from the foundation of the world...

[37] Rom. 4:1-9; Gal. 4:4-5
[38] Gen. 3:15; 1 Cor. 4:10; Heb. 4:2; 1 Pet. 1:10-11
[39] Rev. 13:8
[40] Heb. 13:8

ARTICLE 7

Christ, in the work of mediation, acts according to both natures, by each nature doing that which is proper to itself; yet by reason of the unity of the person, that which is proper to one nature is sometimes in Scripture attributed to the person denominated by the other nature.[41]

[41] John 3:13; Acts 20:28

ARTICLE 8

To all those for whom Christ has obtained eternal redemption, He does certainly and effectually apply and communicate the same;[42] making intercession for them,[43] uniting them to Himself by His Spirit,[44] revealing unto them in and by the Word the mystery of salvation,[45] persuading them to believe and obey,[46] governing their hearts by His Word and Spirit,[47] and overcoming all their enemies by His almighty power and wisdom[48] in such manner and ways as are most consonant to His wonderful and unsearchable dispensation;[49] and all of free and absolute grace, without any condition foreseen in them to procure it.[50]

...governing their hearts by His Word and Spirit...

[42] John 6:37, 39; 10:15-16; 17:9
[43] John 6:37; 10:15-16; 17:9; Rom. 5:10; 8:34; 1 John 2:1-2
[44] Rom. 8:1-2
[45] John 15:13, 15; 17:6; Eph. 1:7-9

[46] John 17:6; Eph. 1:9; 1 John 5:20
[47] John 14:16; 17:17; Rom. 8:9, 14; 15:18-19; 2 Cor. 4:13; Heb. 12:2
[48] Ps. 110:1; 1 Cor. 15:25-26; Col. 2:15
[49] Eph. 1:9-11
[50] John 3:8; Eph. 1:8; 1 John 3:8

ARTICLE 9

This office of mediator between God and man is proper only to Christ, who is the Prophet, Priest, and King of the Church of God; and may not be either in whole or any part thereof transferred from Him to any other.[51]

[51] 1 Tim. 2:5

ARTICLE 10

This number and order of offices is necessary, for in respect of our ignorance, we stand in need of His prophetical office;[52] and in respect of our alienation from God and imperfection of the best of our services, we need His priestly office to reconcile us and present us acceptable unto God;[53] and in respect to our averseness and utter inability to return to God and for our rescue and security from our spiritual adversaries, we need His kingly office to convince, subdue, draw, uphold, deliver, and preserve us to His heavenly kingdom.[54]

...we stand in need of His prophetical office...we need His priestly office...we need His kingly office...

[52] John 1:18
[53] Gal. 5:17; Col. 1:21; Heb. 10:19-21
[54] Ps. 110:3; Luke 1:74-75; John 16:8

Chapter 9

Of Free Will

Chapter 9

ARTICLE 1

God has endued the will of man with that natural liberty and power of acting upon choice that it is neither forced nor by any necessity of nature determined to do good or evil.[1]

[1] Deut. 30:19; Matt. 17:12; Jas. 1:14

ARTICLE 2

Man in his state of innocency had freedom and power to will and to do that which was good and well-pleasing to God;[2] but yet was mutable, so that he might fall from it.[3]

[2] Eccl. 7:29
[3] Gen. 3:6

ARTICLE 3

Man...is not able by his own strength to convert himself or to prepare himself thereunto.

Man by his fall into a state of sin has wholly lost all ability of will to any spiritual good accompanying salvation;[4] so as a natural man, being altogether averse from that good, and dead in sin,[5] is not able by his own strength to convert himself or to prepare himself thereunto.[6]

[4] Rom. 5:6; 8:7
[5] Eph. 2:1-5
[6] Jer. 13:23; Matt. 7:17-18; 12:33-37; Luke 6:43-45; John 1:12-13; 3:3, 5; 5:40; 6:37, 39, 40, 44, 45, 65; 8:31-34; Acts 7:51; 11:18; Rom. 3:10-12; 6:16, 20; 7:18; 8:7; 9:16-18; 1 Cor. 2:14; 2 Cor. 3:14; 4:3-4; Eph. 2:1, 8-9; Phil. 1:29; Tit. 3:3-5; Jas. 1:18

ARTICLE 4

When God converts a sinner and translates him into the state of grace, He frees him from his natural bondage under sin,[7] and by His grace alone, enables him freely to will and to do that which is spiritually good;[8] yet so as that by reason of his remaining corruptions, he does not perfectly nor only will that which is good but does also will that which is evil.[9]

[7] John 8:36; Col. 1:13
[8] John 8:36; Phil. 2:13; Col. 1:13
[9] Rom. 7:14-25; Gal. 5:17

ARTICLE 5

The will of man is made perfectly and immutably free to good alone in the state of glory only.[10]

[10] Eph. 4:13

The will of man is made perfectly and immutably free to good alone in the state of glory only.

Chapter 10

Of Effectual Calling

*Out of great and gross darkness, into marvellous and surprizing
light, 1 Pet. ii.9. God's elect, while in a state of nature, are in a
state of darkness and ignorance; they are in the dark about God,
his perfections, purposes, counsels, and methods of grace; about
themselves, the state and condition they are in; about sin, the nature of
it, and its sad consequences; about the Person of Christ, his offices, and
the way of salvation by him; about the Spirit, his work and operations
on the souls of men; and about the scriptures, and the doctrines of
the gospel contained in them: but in effectual calling the eyes of their
understandings are opened and enlightened,
and they are made light in the Lord.[m]
– John Gill*

Chapter 10

ARTICLE 1

Those whom God[1] has predestinated unto life,[2] He is pleased in His appointed and accepted time,[3] effectually to call[4] by His Word[5] and Spirit,[6] out of that state of sin and death, in which they are by nature, to grace and salvation by Jesus Christ;[7] enlightening their minds spiritually and savingly to understand the things of God;[8] taking away their heart of stone and giving unto them a heart of flesh;[9] renewing their wills; and, by His almighty power, determining them to that which is good; and effectually drawing them to Jesus Christ;[10] yet so as they come most freely, being made willing by His grace.[11]

[1] Rom. 8:28-29

[2] Rom. 8:29-30; 9:22-24; 1 Cor. 1:26-28; 2 Thess. 2:13-14; 2 Tim. 1:9

[3] John 3:8; Eph. 1:11

[4] Ps. 29; Matt. 22:14; John 5:25; Rom. 1:6; 4:17; 8:28, 30; 11:7; 1 Cor. 1:23-24; Eph. 1:10-11; 2 Thess. 2:13, 14; Jude 1

[5] Rom. 1:16-17; 10:14; 2 Thess. 2:14; Heb. 4:12; Jas. 1:17-25; 1 Pet. 1:23-25; 1 John 5:1-5

[6] John 3:3, 5-6, 8; 2 Cor. 3:3, 6

[7] Rom. 8:2; 1 Cor 1:9; Eph. 2:1-6; 2 Tim. 1:9-10

[8] Acts 26:18; Eph. 1:17-18; 1 Cor. 2:10, 12

[9] Ezek. 36:26

[10] Deut. 30:6; Ezek. 36:27; John 6:44-45; Eph. 1:19; Phil. 2:13

[11] Ps. 110:3; Song. 1:4; John 6:37; Rom. 6:16-18

ARTICLE 2

This effectual call is of God's free and special grace alone, not from anything at all foreseen in man nor from any power or agency in the creature[12] coworking with His special grace,[13] the creature being wholly passive therein, being dead in sins and trespasses until being quickened and renewed by the Holy Spirit,[14] he is thereby enabled to answer this call and to embrace the grace offered and conveyed in it; and that by no less power than that which raised up Christ from the dead.[15]

[12] Rom. 9:11; Eph. 2:4-5, 8-9; 2 Tim. 1:9; Tit. 3:4-5
[13] Eph. 2:8; 2 Tim. 1:9
[14] John 5:25; Rom. 8:7; 1 Cor. 2:14; Eph. 2:5
[15] Ezek. 36:27; John 5:25; 6:37; Eph. 1:19-20

ARTICLE 3

Elect infants dying in infancy are regenerated and saved by Christ through the Spirit,[16] who works when and where and how He pleases;[17] so also are all other elect persons who are incapable of being outwardly called by the ministry of the Word.

[16] John 3:3, 5, 6
[17] John 3:8

ARTICLE 4

Others not elected, although they may be called by the ministry of the Word and may have some common operations of the Spirit,[18] yet not being effectually drawn by the Father, they neither will nor can truly come to Christ and therefore cannot be saved;[19] much less can men that receive not the Christian religion be saved,[20]

...yet not being effectually drawn by the Father, they neither will nor can truly come to Christ...

be they never so diligent to frame their lives according to the light of nature and the law of that religion they do profess.[21]

[18] Matt. 7:22; 13:20-21; 22:14; Heb. 6:4-5
[19] John 6:44-45, 65; 1 John 2:24-25
[20] John 6:44-45, 64-66; 8:24
[21] John 4:22; 17:3; Acts 4:12

Chapter 11

Of Justification

Justification is not the making of a person just and righteous, by infusing grace or holiness into him. But it is a discharging him from guilt, and declaring or pronouncing him righteous. So it is a law-term, taken from courts of judicature, wherein a person is accused, tried, and after trial absolved. Thus the scripture opposeth it to accusation and condemnation, Rom. viii. 33, 34. 'Who shall lay any thing to the charge of God's elect? It is God that justifieth: Who is he that condemneth? It is Christ that died, yea rather, that is risen again, who is even at the right hand of God, who also maketh intercession for us,' Deut. xxv.1. 'They shall justify the righteous, and condemn the wicked.' And so it is declared to be a sin to justify the wicked, Prov. xvii.15, not to make them righteous, but to pronounce them righteous.[1]
– Thomas Boston

Chapter 11

ARTICLE 1

Those whom God effectually calls, He also freely justifies,[1] not by infusing righteousness into them, but by pardoning their sins and by accounting and accepting their persons as righteous;[2] not for anything wrought in them or done by them, but for Christ's sake alone;[3] not by imputing faith itself, the act of believing, or any other[4] evangelical obedience to them as their righteousness, but by imputing Christ's active obedience unto the whole Law and passive obedience in His death for their whole and sole righteousness;[4] they receiving and resting on Him and His righteousness by faith; which faith they have not of themselves, it is the gift of God.[5]

[1] Rom. 3:24; 8:30
[2] Rom. 4:5-8; Eph. 1:7
[3] Rom. 5:17-19; 1 Cor. 1:30-31
[4] Eph. 2:8-10; Phil. 3:8-9
[5] Jer. 23:6; John 1:12; Acts 13:38-39; Rom. 3:22-28; 5:17; 2 Cor. 5:19-21; Eph. 2:7-8; Phil. 3:9; Tit. 3:5, 7

ARTICLE 2

Faith thus receiving and resting on Christ and His righteousness is the alone instrument of justification...

Faith thus receiving and resting on Christ and His righteousness is the alone instrument of justification;[6] yet it is not alone in the person justified[7] but is ever accompanied with all other saving graces and is no dead faith but works by love.[8]

[6] Rom. 1:17; 3:27-31; Gal. 3:5; Phil. 3:9
[7] Rom. 8:28
[8] Gal. 5:6; Jas. 2:17, 22, 26

ARTICLE 3

Christ by His obedience and death did fully discharge the debt of all those that are justified and did by the sacrifice of Himself in the blood of His cross, undergoing in their stead the penalty due unto them, make a proper, real, and full satisfaction to God's justice in their behalf;[9] yet inasmuch as He was given by the Father for them[10] and His obedience and satisfaction accepted in their stead,[11] and both freely, not for anything in them,[12] their justification is only of free grace,[13] that both the exact justice and rich grace of God might be glorified in the justification of sinners.[14]

[9] Isa. 53:4-6, 10-12; Rom. 5:8-10, 19; 1 Tim. 2:5-6; Heb. 10:10, 14; 1 Pet. 1:18-19
[10] Rom. 8:32
[11] Matt. 3:17; 2 Cor. 5:21; Eph. 5:2
[12] Rom. 8:32; 2 Cor. 5:21
[13] Rom. 3:24; Eph. 1:7
[14] Rom. 3:26; Eph. 1:6-7; 2:7

ARTICLE 4

God did from all eternity decree to justify all the elect,[15] and Christ did in the fullness of time die for their sins and rise again for their justification;[16] nevertheless they are not justified personally, until the Holy Spirit, does in due time actually apply Christ unto them.[17]

[15] Rom. 8:30; Gal. 3:8; 1 Tim. 2:6; 1 Pet. 1:2, 19-20
[16] Rom. 4:25; Gal. 4:4; 1 Tim. 2:6
[17] Gal. 2:16; Eph. 2:1-3; Col. 1:21-22; Titus 3:4-7

Christ by His obedience and death did fully discharge the debt of all those that are justified...

ARTICLE 5

God does continue to forgive the sins of those that are justified,[18] and although they can never fall from the state of justification,[19] yet they may by their sins fall under God's fatherly displeasure[20] and, in that condition, they have not usually the light of His countenance restored unto them, until they humble themselves, confess their sins, beg pardon, and renew their faith and repentance.[21]

[18] Matt. 6:12; John 13:3-11; 1 John 1:7-2:2
[19] Luke 22:32; John 10:28; Heb. 10:14
[20] Ps. 89:31-33
[21] Ps. 32:5; 51; Matt. 26:75; Luke 1:20

ARTICLE 6

The justification of believers under the Old Testament was, in all these respects, one and the same with the justification of believers under the New Testament.[22]

[22] Rom. 4:22-24; Gal. 3:9

Chapter 12

Of Adoption

*Let me mention to you a second part of the blessedness we get. The
Spirit of the Son dwells in us. You will see this in Galatians 4.6,
"Because ye are sons, God hath sent forth the Spirit of his Son into
your hearts, crying, Abba, Father." Brethren, when Christ comes, the
first thing he does is to redeem you from under the curse of the law,
and then he makes you a son. O it is sweet to have the smile of Christ!
it is sweet to get the love of Christ; but I will tell you what is equally
as sweet? that is to receive the Spirit of Christ. Has he given you the
Spirit? He will do it if you are a son, that you may be made to cry,
"Abba, Father."[b]*
– Robert Murray M'Cheyne

Chapter 12

All those that are justified, God vouchsafed, in and for the sake of His only Son Jesus Christ, to make partakers of the grace of adoption...

All those that are justified,[1] God vouchsafed,[2] in and for the sake of His only Son Jesus Christ,[3] to make partakers of the grace of adoption;[4] by which they are taken into the number and enjoy the liberties and privileges of children of God; have His name put upon them;[5] receive the Spirit of adoption; have access to the throne of grace with boldness; are enabled to cry Abba, Father;[6] are pitied, protected, provided for, and chastened by Him, as by a Father; yet never cast off, but sealed to the day of redemption[7] and inherit the promises as heirs of everlasting salvation.[8]

[1] Gal. 3:24-26
[2] 1 John 3:1-3
[3] Rom. 8:17, 29; Gal. 4:4-5; Eph. 1:5
[4] Gal. 4:4-5; Eph. 1:5
[5] John 1:12; Rom. 8:17; 2 Cor. 6:18; Rev. 3:12
[6] Rom. 5:2; 8:15; Gal. 4:6; Eph. 2:18; 3:12
[7] Ps. 103:13; Pro. 14:26; Isa. 54:8-9; Lam. 3:31; Matt. 6:30, 32; Eph. 4:30; Heb. 12:6; 1 Pet. 5:7
[8] Rom. 8:17; Heb. 1:14; 6:12; 9:15

Chapter 13

Of Sanctification

The fact of the matter is that very much of that which now passes for sanctification is nothing but a species of pharisaism, which causes its deluded votaries to thank God that they are not like other men; and sad it is to find many of the Lord's people adding to their miseries by grieving over how far they come behind the lofty attainments which they imagine these boasters have reached unto. A true and God-honoring 'Christian testimony', my reader, does not consist in magnifying self, by telling of attainments and excellencies which, with apparent humility, are ascribed to divine enabling. No indeed, very far from it. That 'witness' which is most honoring to the Lord is one which acknowledges his amazing grace and which magnifies his infinite patience in continuing to bear with such an ungrateful, hard-hearted, and unresponsive wretch.[p]
– A. W. Pink

Chapter 13

ARTICLE 1

They who are united to Christ, effectually called and regenerated, having a new heart and a new spirit created in them through the virtue of Christ's death and resurrection,[1] are also farther sanctified, really and personally,[2] through the same virtue,[3] by His Word and Spirit dwelling in them;[4] the dominion of the whole body of sin is destroyed,[5] and the several lusts thereof are more and more weakened and mortified;[6] and they more and more quickened and strengthened in all saving graces[7] to the practice of all true holiness,[8] without which no man shall see the Lord.[9]

[1] John 3:3-8; Acts 20:32; 26:18; Rom. 1:7; 6:1-11; 15:16; 1 Cor. 1:2, 6:11; 2 Cor. 1:1; Eph. 1:1; Phil. 1:1; Col. 3:12; 1 John 2:29; 3:9-10
[2] Acts 20:32; Rom. 6:5-6, 19, 22; 1 Thess. 5:23
[3] Acts 20:32; Rom. 6:5-6; 1 Cor. 6:11; Phil. 3:10
[4] John 17:17; Rom. 8:13; Eph. 3:16-19; 5:26; 1 Thess. 5:21-23;
[5] Rom. 6:14
[6] Gal. 5:24
[7] Col. 1:11
[8] 2 Cor. 7:1; Heb. 12:14

ARTICLE 2

This sanctification is throughout, in the whole man, yet imperfect in this life; there abides still some remnants of corruption in every part,[9] whence arises a continual and irreconcilable war:[10] the flesh lusting against the Spirit and the Spirit against the flesh.[11]

[9] Rom. 7:18, 23; Phil. 3:12; 1 Thess. 5:23; 1 John 1:8, 10
[10] 1 Cor. 9:24-27; 1 Tim. 1:18; 6:12; 2 Tim. 4:7
[11] Gal. 5:17; 1 Pet. 2:11

Article 3

In which war, although the remaining corruption for a time may much prevail,[12] yet through the continual supply of strength from the sanctifying Spirit of Christ, the regenerate part does overcome;[13] and so the saints grow in grace, perfecting holiness in the fear of God, pressing after a heavenly life in evangelical obedience to all the commands which Christ as Head and King in His Word has prescribed to them.[14]

[12] Rom. 7:23
[13] Rom. 6:14; Eph. 4:15-16; 1 John 5:4
[14] Matt. 28:20; 2 Cor. 3:18; 7:1; Eph. 4:15-16; 2 Pet. 3:18

...through the continual supply of strength from the sanctifying Spirit of Christ, the regenerate part does overcome...

Chapter 14

Of Saving Faith

In this final message on Faith, I desire by the grace of God and the Holy Spirit working in us, to look with you at the one expression in God's Word that more than any other, characterizes the subject we have been endeavoring to lay before your hearts these many weeks: It is the expression found in Heb. 12:2 which reads, "LOOKING UNTO JESUS" the secret of the Christian life, the life that is in the Lord Jesus Christ, the life of faith, whereby we are saved, justified, sanctified, kept, and comforted; by which also we overcome the world, sin and Satan and persevere to the end.[q]
– L. R. Shelton, Jr.

Chapter 14

ARTICLE 1

The grace of faith, whereby the elect are enabled to believe to the saving of their souls, is the work of the Spirit of Christ in their hearts[1] and is ordinarily wrought by the ministry of the Word;[2] by which also and by the administration of baptism and the Lord's Supper, prayer, and other means appointed of God, it is increased and strengthened.[3]

[1] 2 Cor. 4:13; Eph. 2:8

[2] John 6:37, 44; Acts 11:21, 24; 13:48; 14:27; 15:9; Rom. 10:14, 17; 2 Cor. 4:13; Eph. 2:8; Phil. 1:29; 2 Thess. 2:13; 1 Pet. 1:2

[3] Luke 17:5; Acts 20:32; Rom. 4:11; 10:14, 17; 1 Pet. 2:2

ARTICLE 2

By this faith, a Christian believes to be true whatsoever is revealed in the Word for the authority of God Himself,[4] and also apprehends an excellency therein above all other writings and all things in the world,[5] as it bears forth the glory of God in His attributes, the excellency of Christ in His nature and offices, and the power and fullness of the Holy Spirit in His workings and operations; and so is enabled to cast his soul upon the truth thus believed;[6] and also acts differently upon that which each particular passage thereof contains: yielding obedience to the commands,[7] trembling at the threatenings,[8] and embracing the promises of God for this life and that which is to come;[9] but the principal acts of saving faith have immediate relation to Christ: accepting, receiving, and resting upon Him alone for justification, sanctification, and eternal life, by virtue of the Covenant of Grace.[10]

[4] Acts 24:14
[5] Ps. 27:7-10; 119:72
[6] Ps. 19:7-10; 119:72; Acts 24:14; 1 Thess. 2:13; 2 Tim. 1:12
[7] John 14:14; 15:14; Rom. 8:26
[8] Isa. 66:2
[9] 1 Tim. 4:8; Heb. 11:13
[10] John 1:12; Acts 15:11; 16:31; Gal. 2:20

ARTICLE 3

This faith although it be different in degrees and may be weak or strong,[11] yet it is, in the least degree of it, different in the kind or nature of it (as is all other saving grace) from the faith and common grace of temporary believers;[12] and therefore though it may be many times assailed and weakened, yet it gets the victory;[13] growing up in many to the attainment of a full assurance[14] through Christ,[15] who is both the Author and Finisher of our faith.[16]

> ...yet it gets the victory...

[11] Matt. 6:30; 8:10, 26; 14:31; 16:8; 17:20; Rom. 4:19-20; Heb. 5:13-14
[12] Jas. 2:14; 2 Pet. 1:1; 1 John 5:4
[13] Luke 22:31-32; Eph. 6:16; 1 John 5:4-5
[14] Ps. 119:114; Heb. 6:11-12; 10:22-23
[15] Col. 2:2; Heb. 6:11-12
[16] Heb. 12:2

Chapter 15

Of Repentance unto Life and Salvation

*[Repentance] is, in a word, the turning of a man to God. For by
nature we are alienated from God and can do nothing but the things
he condemns...Now here is God calling us to himself by repentance...
we see repentance does not lie in outward nonsensical actions, such as
abstaining from eating meats on one day rather than on another and
engaging in a thousand other monkey tricks like those performed by
the Papacy. But repentance has its set in the spirit and in the heart.
That is why we must pay close attention to what we have touched on.
For when we come to God, will we come with feet or hands or tongue?
Not at all! The heart must work at it. And in fact, this word,
as used in Scripture tells us mainly that we have become
new creatures (2 Cor 5:17).*[r]
– John Calvin

Chapter 15

ARTICLE 1

Such of the elect as are converted at riper years, having sometimes lived in the state of nature and therein served divers lusts and pleasures, God, in their effectual calling, gives them repentance unto life.[1]

[1] 2 Chr. 33:10-20; Acts 9:1-19; 16:29-30; Tit. 3:2-5

ARTICLE 2

...there is none that does good and sins not...

Whereas there is none that does good and sins not,[2] and the best of men may through the power and deceitfulness of their corruption dwelling in them, with the prevalence of temptation, fall into great sins and provocations;[3] God has, in the Covenant of Grace, mercifully provided that believers so sinning and falling be renewed through repentance unto salvation.[4]

[2] Ps. 130:3; 143:2; Pro. 20:9; Eccl. 7:20
[3] 2 Sam. 11:1-27; Luke 22:54-62
[4] Jer. 32:40; Luke 22:31-32; 1 John 1:9

ARTICLE 3

This saving repentance is an evangelical grace,[5] whereby a person, being by the Holy Spirit made sensible of the manifold evils of his sin,[6] does, by faith in Christ,[7] humble himself for it with godly sorrow, detestation of it, and self-abhorrency;[8] praying for pardon and strength of grace;[9] with a purpose and endeavor, by supplies of the Spirit, to walk before God, unto all well pleasing in all things.[10]

[5] Zech. 12:10; Acts 5:31; 11:18; 2 Tim. 2:25
[6] Ps. 51:1-6; 130:1-3; Luke 15:17-20; Acts 2:37-38
[7] Ps. 130:4; Matt. 27:3-5; Mark 1:15
[8] Ezek. 36:31; 2 Cor. 7:11
[9] Ezek. 16:60-63; 36:31-32; Zech. 12:10; Matt. 21:29; Acts 15:18; 20:21; 26:20; 2 Cor. 7:10-11; 1 Thess. 1:9
[10] Ps. 119:6, 59, 104, 128; Pro. 28:13; Ezek. 36:25; 18:30-31; Matt. 3:8; Luke 3:8; Acts 26:20; 1 Thess. 1:9

ARTICLE 4

As repentance is to be continued through the whole course of our lives upon the account of the body of death and the motions thereof,[11] so it is every man's duty to repent of his particular known sins particularly.[12]

...it is every man's duty, to repent of his particular known sins particularly.

[11] Ezek. 16:60; Matt. 5:4; 1 John 1:9
[12] Luke 19:8; 1 Tim. 1:13, 15

ARTICLE 5

Such is the provision which God has made through Christ in the Covenant of Grace for the preservation of believers unto salvation that although there is no sin so small but it deserves damnation,[13] yet there is no sin so great that it shall bring damnation on them that repent, which makes the constant preaching of repentance necessary.[14]

[13] Ps. 130:3; 143:2; Rom. 6:23
[14] Isa. 1:16-18; 55:7; Acts 2:36-38

Chapter 16

Of Good Works

*So we say, good works are the best evidence of spiritual life in the soul.
Is it not written, "We know that we have passed from death unto life,
because we love the brethren?" Loving the brethren is a good work.
Again, "If any man abide in me, he shall bring forth fruit." Fruits of
righteousness are good works, and they are evidence that we abide in
Christ. If I am living in sin day by day, what right have I to
conclude I am a child of God?*[8]
– Charles Spurgeon

Chapter 16

Good works
are only such
as God has
commanded
in His Holy
Word...

ARTICLE 1

Good works are only such as God has commanded in His Holy Word,[1] and not such as, without the warrant thereof, are devised by men, out of blind zeal or upon any pretense of good intentions.[2]

[1] Mic. 6:8; Rom. 12:2; Col. 2:3; 2 Tim. 3:16-17; Heb. 13:21
[2] 1 Sam. 15:21-23; Isa. 29:13; Matt. 15:9; John 16:2; Rom. 10:2; 1 Cor. 7:23; Gal. 5:1; Col. 2:8, 16-23; 1 Pet. 1:18

ARTICLE 2

These good works, done in obedience to God's commandments, are the fruits and evidences of a true and lively faith;[3] and by them, believers manifest their thankfulness,[4] strengthen their assurance,[5] edify their brethren,[6] adorn the profession of the Gospel,[7] stop the mouths of the adversaries,[8] and glorify God,[9] whose workmanship they are, created in Christ Jesus thereunto,[10] that having their fruit unto holiness, they may have the end eternal life.[11]

[3] Gal. 5:26; 1 Tim. 1:5; Jas. 2:18, 22
[4] Ps. 116:12-14; Matt. 26:1-11; Luke 7:36-50; 1 Pet. 2:9, 12
[5] 2 Pet. 1:5-11; 1 John 2:3, 5; 3:18-19
[6] Matt. 5:16; 2 Cor. 9:2
[7] Matt. 5:16; 1 Tim. 6:1; Tit. 2:5, 9-12; 1 Pet. 2:12
[8] 1 Tim. 6:1; Tit. 2:5; 1 Pet. 2:12, 15
[9] Phil. 1:11; 1 Tim. 6:1; 1 Pet. 2:15
[10] Matt. 5:16; Eph. 2:10; Phil. 1:11; 1 Tim. 6:1; 1 Pet. 2:12
[11] Matt. 7:13-14, 21-23; Rom. 6:22

ARTICLE 3

Their ability to do good works is not at all of themselves but wholly from the Spirit of Christ;[12] and that they may be enabled thereunto, besides the graces they have already received, there is necessary an actual influence of the same Holy Spirit to work in them to will and to do of His good pleasure;[13] yet are they not hereupon to grow negligent, as if they were not bound to perform any duty unless upon a special motion of the Spirit; but they ought to be diligent in stirring up the grace of God that is in them.[14]

[12] John 15:4-5
[13] Ezek. 36:26-27; John 15:4-6; 2 Cor. 3:5; Eph. 2:10; Phil. 2:12-13
[14] Isa. 64:7; Rom. 8:14; John 3:8; Phil. 2:12-13; 2 Tim. 1:6; Heb. 6:11-12; 2 Pet. 1:10;Jude 20-21

...wholly from the Spirit of Christ...

ARTICLE 4

They, who in their obedience attain to the greatest height which is possible in this life, are so far from being able to supererogate and to do more than God requires, as that they fall short of much which in duty they are bound to do.[15]

[15] 1 Kgs 8:46; 2 Chr. 6:36; Job 9:2-3; Ps. 130:3; 143:2; Pro. 20:9; Eccl. 7:20; Luke 17:10; Rom. 3:9, 23; 7:14f.; Gal. 5:17; 1 John 1:6-10

ARTICLE 5

We cannot by our best works merit pardon of sin or eternal life at the hand of God by reason of the great disproportion that is between them and the glory to come[16] and the infinite distance that is between us and God, whom, by them, we can neither profit nor satisfy for the debt of our former sins;[17] but when we have done all we can, we have done but our duty and are unprofitable servants;[18] and because, as they are good, they proceed from His Spirit,[19] and, as they are wrought by us, they are defiled and mixed with so much weakness and imperfection that they cannot endure the severity of God's judgment.[20]

[16] Rom. 8:18
[17] Rom. 3:20; 4:6; Eph. 2:8-9
[18] Job 22:3; 35:7; Luke 17:10; Rom. 4:3; 11:3
[19] Gal. 5:22-23
[20] 1 Kgs. 8:46; 2 Chr. 6:36; Ps. 130:3; 143:2; Pro. 20:9; Eccl. 7:20; Isa. 64:6; Rom. 3:9, 23; 7:14f.; Gal. 5:17; 1 John 1:6-10

ARTICLE 6

...is pleased to accept and reward that which is sincere, although accompanied with many weaknesses and imperfections.

Yet notwithstanding the persons of believers being accepted through Christ, their good works also are accepted in Him;[21] not as though they were in this life wholly unblameable and unreprovable in God's sight;[22] but that He, looking upon them in His Son, is pleased to accept and reward that which is sincere, although accompanied with many weaknesses and imperfections.[23]

[21] Exo. 28:38; Eph. 1:6-7; 1 Pet. 2:5
[22] 1 Kgs. 8:46; 2 Chr. 6:36; Ps. 130:3; 143:2; Pro. 20:9; Eccl. 7:20; Rom. 3:9, 23; 7:14f.; Gal. 5:17; 1 John 1:6-10
[23] Matt. 25:21, 23; Heb. 6:10

ARTICLE 7

Works done by unregenerate men although for the matter of them they may be things which God commands and of good use both to themselves and others;[24] yet because they proceed not from a heart purified by faith[25] nor are done in a right manner according to the Word[26] nor to a right end – the glory of God,[27] they are therefore sinful and cannot please God nor make a man meet to receive grace from God;[28] and yet their neglect of them is more sinful and displeasing to God.[29]

[24] 1 Kgs. 21:27-29; 2 Kgs. 10:30-31; Rom. 2:14; Phil. 1:15-18
[25] Gen. 4:5; Rom. 14:23; Gal. 5:6; 1 Tim. 1:5; Heb. 11:4-6
[26] Isa. 1:12; 1 Cor. 13:1, 3
[27] Matt. 6:2, 5-6; 1 Cor. 10:31
[28] Amos 5:21-22; Rom. 9:16; Tit. 1:15; 3:5
[29] 1 Kgs. 21:27-29; 2 Kgs. 10:30-31; Ps. 14:4; 36:3; Job 21:14-15; Matt. 25:41-43

Works done by unregenerate men...are... sinful and cannot please God.

Chapter 17

Of Perseverance of the Saints

The doctrine of the saints final perseverance in grace to glory, being a doctrine so fully expressed in the sacred scriptures, so clearly wrote there as with a sun-beam, having so large a compass of proof; as scarce any other doctrine has; a doctrine so agreeable to the perfections of God, and the contrary so manifestly reflecting dishonor upon them, particularly the immutability of God, his wisdom, power, goodness, justice, truth, and faithfulness; a doctrine so well established upon his purposes and decrees, his counsel and covenant, and which so well accords with all his acts of grace towards, and upon his people; a doctrine so well calculated for their spiritual peace and comfort, and to promote holiness of life and conversation...[1]
– John Gill

Chapter 17

ARTICLE 1

…shall certainly persevere therein to the end and be eternally saved…

Those whom God has accepted in the beloved, effectually called and sanctified by His Spirit, and given the precious faith of His elect unto can neither totally nor finally fall from the state of grace, but shall certainly persevere therein to the end and be eternally saved, seeing the gifts and callings of God are without repentance (whence He still begets and nourishes in them faith, repentance, love, joy, hope, and all the graces of the Spirit unto immortality),[1] and though many storms and floods arise and beat against them, yet they shall never be able to take them off that foundation and rock which by faith they are fastened upon; notwithstanding through unbelief and the temptations of Satan, the sensible sight of the light and love of God may for a time be clouded and obscured from them,[2] yet He is still the same and they shall be sure to be kept by the power of God unto salvation, where they shall enjoy their purchased possession, they being engraven upon the palm of His hands and their names having been written in the book of life from all eternity.[3]

[1] John 10:28-29; Phil. 1:6; 2 Tim. 2:19; 2 Pet. 1:5-10; 1 John 2:19
[2] Ps. 89:31-32; 1 Cor. 11:32; 2 Tim. 4:7
[3] Ps. 102:27; Mal. 3:6; Eph. 1:14; 1 Pet. 1:5; Rev. 13:8

ARTICLE 2

This perseverance of the saints depends not upon their own free will[4] but upon the immutability of the decree of election[5] flowing from the free and unchangeable love of God the Father, upon the efficacy of the merit and intercession of Jesus Christ and union with Him,[6] the oath of God,[7] the abiding of His Spirit, and the seed of God within them,[8] and the nature of the Covenant of Grace,[9] from all which arises also the certainty and infallibility thereof.

...from all which arises also the certainty and infallibility thereof.

[4] John 6:37, 44; Rom. 9:16; Phil. 2:12-13
[5] Matt. 24:22, 24, 31; Rom. 8:30; 9:11, 16; 11:2, 29; Eph. 1:5-11
[6] John 14:19; 10:28-29; Rom. 5:9-10; 8:31-38; 1 Cor. 1:8-9; 2 Cor. 5:14; Eph. 1:4
[7] Heb. 6:16-20
[8] 2 Cor. 1:22; 5:5; Eph. 1:13-14; 4:30; 1 John 2:19-20, 27; 3:9; 5:4, 18
[9] Jer. 31:33-34; 32:40; Heb. 10:11-18; 13:20-21

ARTICLE 3

And though they may, through the temptation of Satan and of the world, the prevalency of corruption remaining in them, and the neglect of means of their preservation, fall into grievous sins and for a time continue therein,[10] whereby they incur God's displeasure and grieve His Holy Spirit,[11] come to have their graces and comforts impaired,[12] have their hearts hardened and their consciences wounded,[13] hurt, and scandalize others,[14] and bring temporal judgments upon themselves;[15] yet they shall renew their repentance and be preserved through faith in Christ Jesus to the end.[16]

[10] Matt. 26:70, 72, 74
[11] Ps. 38:1-8; Isa. 54:5-9; 64:5, 9; Eph. 4:30; 1 Thess. 5:14
[12] Ps. 51:10-12
[13] Ps. 32:3-4; 73:21-22
[14] 2 Sam. 12:14; Rom. 14:13-18; 1 Cor. 8:9-13; 1 Tim. 6:1-2; Tit. 2:5
[15] Gen. 19:30-38; 2 Sam. 12:14f.; 1 Cor. 11:27-32
[16] Luke 22:32, 61-62; 1 Cor. 11:32; 1 John 3:9; 5:18

Chapter 18

Of Assurance of Grace and Salvation

Believe me, believe me, assurance is worth the seeking. You forsake your own mercies when you rest content without it. The things I speak are for your peace. If it is good to be sure in earthly things, how much better is it to be sure in heavenly things! Your salvation is a fixed and certain thing. God knows it... Make it then your daily prayer that you may have an increase of faith. According to your faith will be your peace. Cultivate that blessed root more, and sooner or later, by God's blessing, you may hope to have the flower, You may not perhaps attain to full assurance all at once. It is good sometimes to be kept waiting: we do not value things which we get without trouble. But though it tarry, wait for it. Seek on, and expect to find.[ii]
– J. C. Ryle

Chapter 18

Article 1

Although temporary believers and other unregenerate men may vainly deceive themselves with false hopes and carnal presumptions of being in the favor of God and state of salvation, which hope of theirs shall perish;[1] yet such as truly believe in the Lord Jesus and love Him in sincerity, endeavoring to walk in all good conscience before Him, may in this life be certainly assured that they are in the state of grace and may rejoice in the hope of the glory of God,[2] which hope shall never make them ashamed.[3]

[1] Job 8:13-14; Jer. 17:9; Matt. 7:21-23; Luke 18:10-14; John 8:41; Gal. 6:3, 7-9; Eph. 5:6-7
[2] 1 John 2:3; 3:14, 18-19, 21, 24; 5:13
[3] Rom. 5:2, 5; 8:16; 2 Pet. 1:10; 1 John 2:3, 3:14, 18-19, 24, 5:13

Article 2

...but an infallible assurance of faith founded on the blood and righteousness of Christ revealed in the Gospel...

This certainty is not a bare conjectural and probable persuasion grounded upon a fallible hope, but an infallible assurance of faith[4] founded on the blood and righteousness of Christ revealed in the Gospel[5] and also upon the inward evidence of those graces of the Spirit unto which promises are made[6] and on the testimony of the Spirit of adoption witnessing with our spirits that we are the children of God;[7] and as a fruit thereof, keeping the heart both humble and holy.[8]

[4] Rom. 5:2, 5; Heb. 6:11, 19-20; 1 John 3:2, 14; 4:16; 5:13, 19-20
[5] Heb. 6:17-18; 7:22; 10:14, 19

[6] Matt. 3:7-10; Mark 1:15; 2 Pet. 1:4-11; 1 John 2:3; 3:14, 18-19, 24; 5:13
[7] Rom. 8:15-16; 1 Cor. 2:12; Gal. 4:6-7
[8] 1 John 3:1-3

ARTICLE 3

This infallible assurance does not so belong to the essence of faith but that a true believer may wait long and conflict with many difficulties before he be partaker of it;[9] yet being enabled by the Spirit to know the things which are freely given him of God, he may without extraordinary revelation in the right use of means attain thereunto;[10] and therefore it is the duty of everyone to give all diligence to make their calling and election sure, that thereby his heart may be enlarged in peace and joy in the Holy Spirit, in love and thankfulness to God, and in strength and cheerfulness in the duties of obedience, the proper fruits of this assurance;[11] so far is it from inclining men to looseness.[12]

...being enabled by the Spirit to know the things which are freely given him of God...

[9] Ps. 77:1-12; Ps. 88; Isa. 50:10; Acts 16:30-34; 1 John 5:13
[10] Rom. 8:15-16; 1 Cor. 2:12; Gal. 3:2; 4:4-6; Eph. 3:17-19; Heb. 6:11-12; 2 Pet. 1:5-11; 1 John 4:13
[11] Ps. 119:32; Rom. 5:1-2, 5; 14:17
[12] Neh. 8:10; Ps. 119:32; Rom. 6:1-2, 11-13; 14:17; 15:13; 2; Tit. 2:11-14; 2 Pet. 1:10; 1 John 4:16, 19

ARTICLE 4

True believers may have the assurance of their salvation divers ways shaken, diminished, and intermitted; as by negligence in preserving of it,[13] by falling into some special sin, which wounds the conscience and grieves the Spirit,[14] by some sudden or vehement temptation,[15] by God's withdrawing the light of His countenance and suffering even such as fear Him to walk in darkness and to have no light;[16] yet are they never destitute of the seed of God and life of faith, that love of Christ and the brethren, that sincerity of heart and conscience of duty, out of which, by the operation of the Spirit, this assurance may in due time be revived and, by the which in the mean time, they are preserved from utter despair.[17]

...yet are they never destitute...

[13] Song. 5:2-3, 6; Heb. 6:11-12; 2 Pet. 1:5-11
[14] Ps. 51:8, 12, 14; Eph. 4:30
[15] Ps. 30:7; 31:22; 77:7-8; 116:11
[16] Ps. 30:7; Isa. 50:10
[17] Ps. 42:5, 11; Lam. 3:26-31; Luke 22:32; Rom. 8:15-16; Gal. 4:5; 1 John 3:9

Chapter 19

Of the Law of God

[A Christian] takes a sweet complacent delight in the law. 'I delight in the law of God after the inward man.' Rom. vii 22....'O! how love I thy law.' Psa cxix 97. Though a Christian cannot keep God's law, yet he loves his law; though he cannot serve God perfectly, yet he serves him willingly...It is his cordial desire to walk in all God's commands. 'O that my ways were directed to keep thy statues.' Psa cxix 5. Though his strength fails, yet his pulse beats....He really endeavours to obey God's law perfectly; and wherein he comes short he runs to Christ's blood to supply his defects.[v]
– Thomas Watson

Chapter 19

ARTICLE 1

God gave to Adam a law of universal obedience written in his heart[1] and a particular precept of not eating the fruit of the tree of knowledge of good and evil;[2] by which He bound him and all his posterity to personal, entire, exact, and perpetual obedience; promised life upon the fulfilling; and threatened death upon the breach of it; and endued him with power and ability to keep it.[3]

[1] Gen. 1:27; Eccl. 7:29; Rom. 2:12a, 14-15
[2] Gen. 1:27; 2:16-17; Eccl. 7:29
[3] Gen. 2:16-17; Rom. 10:5; Gal. 3:10, 12

ARTICLE 2

The same law that was first written in the heart of man continued to be a perfect rule of righteousness after the Fall[4] and was delivered by God upon Mount Sinai[5] in Ten Commandments and written in two tables – the four first containing our duty towards God and the other six our duty to man.[6]

The same law that was first written in the heart of man continued to be a perfect rule of righteousness after the Fall...

[4] Rom. 2:14-15; For the Fourth Commandment, Gen. 2:3; Exo. 16; Gen. 7:4; 8:10, 12; for the Fifth Commandment, Gen. 37:10; for the Sixth Commandment, Gen. 4:3-15; for the Seventh Commandment, Gen. 12:17; for the Eighth Commandment, Gen. 31:30; 44:8; for the Ninth Commandment, Gen. 27:12; for the Tenth Commandment, Gen. 6:2; 13:10-11
[5] Rom. 2:12a, 14-15
[6] Exo. 32:15-16; 34:4, 28; Deut. 10:4

ARTICLE 3

Besides this law commonly called moral, God was pleased to give to the people of Israel ceremonial laws: containing several typical ordinances partly of worship; prefiguring Christ – His graces, actions, sufferings, and benefits;[7] and partly holding forth divers instructions of moral duties,[8] all which ceremonial laws, being appointed only to the time of reformation, are by Jesus Christ the true Messiah and only Lawgiver, who was furnished with power from the Father for that end, abrogated and taken away.[9]

[7] Col. 2:16-17; Heb. 10:1
[8] 1 Cor. 5:7; 2 Cor. 6:17; Jude 23
[9] Eph. 2:14-16; Col. 2:14, 16-17

ARTICLE 4

To them also He gave sundry judicial laws, which expired together with the state of that people, not obliging any now by virtue of that institution;[10] their general equity only being of moral use.[11]

[10] Luke 21:20-24; Acts 6:13-14; Heb. 9:18-19 with 8:7, 13; 9:10; 10:1
[11] 1 Cor. 5:1; 9:8-10

ARTICLE 5

The moral law does forever bind all, as well justified persons as others, to the obedience thereof,[12] and that not only in regard of the matter contained in it but also in respect of the authority of God the Creator who gave

The moral law does forever bind all…

it;[13] neither does Christ in the Gospel any way dissolve but much strengthen this obligation.[14]

[12] Matt. 19:16-22; Rom. 2:14-15; 3:19-20; 6:14; 7:6; 8:3; 13:8-10; 1 Cor. 7:19 with Gal. 5:6; 6:15; Eph. 4:25-6:4; 1 Tim. 1:8-11; Jas. 2:8, 10-12

[13] Jas. 2:10-11

[14] Matt. 5:17-19; Rom. 3:31; 1 Cor. 9:21; Jas. 2:8

ARTICLE 6

Although true believers be not under the Law, as a Covenant of Works to be thereby justified or condemned,[15] yet it is of great use to them as well as to others; in that, as a rule of life, informing them of the will of God and their duty, it directs and binds them to walk accordingly;[16] discovering also the sinful pollutions of their natures, hearts, and lives; so as examining themselves thereby, they may come to further conviction of, humiliation for, and hatred against sin;[17] together with a clearer sight of the need they have of Christ and the perfection of His obedience.[18] It is likewise of use to the regenerate to restrain their corruptions in that it forbids sin; and the threatenings of it serve to show what even their sins deserve and what afflictions in this life they may expect for them, although freed from the curse and unallayed rigor thereof.[19] The promises of it likewise show them God's approbation of obedience and what blessings they may expect upon the performance thereof,[20] though not as due to them by the Law as a Covenant of Works,[21] so as man's doing good and refraining from evil, because the Law encourages to the one and deters from the other, is no evidence of his being under the Law and not under grace.[22]

...as a rule of life, informing them of the will of God and their duty, it directs and binds them to walk accordingly...

[15] Acts 13:39; Rom. 6:14; 8:1; 10:4; Gal. 2:16; 4:4-5

[16] Ps. 119:4-6; Rom. 7:12, 22, 25; 1 Cor. 7:19

[17] Rom. 3:20; 7:7, etc.

[18] Rom. 3:20; 7:7, 9, 14, 24, 8:3; Jas. 1:23-25

[19] Ps. 119:101, 104, 128; Jas. 2:11

[20] Ps. 19:11; 37:11; Matt. 5:6; Eph. 6:2-3

[21] Luke 17:10

[22] See the book of Proverbs; Matt. 3:7; Luke 13:3, 5; Acts 2:40; Rom. 6:12-14; 1 Pet. 3:8-13; Heb. 11:26

ARTICLE 7

Neither are the forementioned uses of the Law contrary to the grace of the Gospel but do sweetly comply with it, the Spirit of Christ subduing and enabling the will of man to do that freely and cheerfully which the will of God, revealed in the Law, requires to be done.[23]

...the Spirit of Christ subduing and enabling the will of man...

[23] Jer. 31:33; Ezek. 36:27; Rom. 8:4; Gal. 3:21; Tit. 2:14

Chapter 20

Of the Gospel and of the Extent of the Grace Thereof

Accept, then, the character of God as given in the gospel; read aright his blessed name as it is written upon the cross; take the simple interpretation given of his mind toward the ungodly, as you have it, at length, in the glad tidings of peace. Is not that enough? If that which God has made known of himself be not enough to allay your fears, nothing else will. The Holy Spirit will not give you peace, irrespective of your views of God's character. That would be countenancing the worship of a false god, instead of the true God revealed in the Bible. It is in connection with the truth concerning the true God, "the God of all grace," that the Spirit gives peace. It is the love of the true God that he sheds abroad in the heart.[w]

– Horatius Bonar

Chapter 20

ARTICLE 1

The Covenant of Works being broken by sin and made unprofitable unto life, God was pleased to give forth the promise of Christ, the seed of the woman, as the means of calling the elect and begetting in them faith and repentance; in this promise, the Gospel, as to the substance of it, was revealed and [is] therein effectual for the conversion and salvation of sinners.[1]

[1] Gen. 3:15; Luke 2:25, 38; 23:51; Rom. 4:13-16; Gal. 3:15-22; 4:4; Eph. 2:12; Heb. 11:13; Rev. 13:8

ARTICLE 2

This promise of Christ and salvation by Him is revealed only by the Word of God;[2] neither do the works of creation or providence with the light of nature make discovery of Christ or of grace by Him so much as in a general or obscure way;[3] much less that men, destitute of the revelation of Him by the promise or Gospel, should be enabled thereby to attain saving faith or repentance.[4]

This promise of Christ and salvation by Him is revealed only by the Word of God...

[2] Acts 4:12; Rom. 1:17; 10:13-15
[3] Ps. 19; Rom. 1:18-23; 10:14, 15, 17
[4] Pro. 29:18; Isa. 25:7; 60:2-3; Matt. 28:18-20; Luke 24:46-47; Acts 17:29-30; Rom. 2:12a; 3:9-20

ARTICLE 3

The revelation of the Gospel unto sinners made in divers times and by sundry parts with the addition of promises and precepts for the obedience required therein, as to the nations and persons to whom it is granted, is merely of the sovereign will and good pleasure of God,[5] not being annexed by virtue of any promise to the due improvement of men's natural abilities by virtue of common light received without it, which none ever did make or can so do;[6] and therefore in all ages, the preaching of the Gospel has been granted unto persons and nations, as to the extent or straightening of it, in great variety, according to the counsel of the will of God.

[5] Ps. 147:20; Matt. 11:20; Acts 16:7
[6] Rom. 1:18-32; 3:10-12; 8:7-8

ARTICLE 4

Although the Gospel be the only outward means of revealing Christ and saving grace; and is, as such, abundantly sufficient thereunto;[7] yet that men who are dead in trespasses may be born again, quickened, or regenerated there is moreover necessary an effectual, insuperable work of the Holy Spirit upon the whole soul, for the producing in them a new spiritual life,[8] without which, no other means will effect their conversion unto God.[9]

...there is moreover necessary an effectual, insuperable work of the Holy Spirit...

[7] Rom. 1:16-17
[8] Ps. 110:3; 1 Cor. 2:14; Eph. 1:19-20
[9] John 6:44; 1 Cor. 1:22-24; 2:14; 2 Cor. 4:4, 6

Chapter 21

Of Christian Liberty and Liberty of Conscience

But though it is not to be wondered at, it is to be deeply deplored that some, whom we have good reasons to look upon as the Lord's servants, should be found lending themselves to forwarding this incoming tide of spiritual anarchy. The Word of truth declares that "grace reigns through righteousness" (Rom. 5:21), not at the expense of it; and there can be no righteousness apart from law. Righteousness is right doing; and right doing is conformity to law. The only other alternative is what the writer of the book of Judges speaks of, namely, "Every man doing that which was right in his own eyes" (21:25), which is a state of anarchy.[x]
– A. W. Pink

Chapter 21

ARTICLE 1

The liberty which Christ has purchased for believers under the Gospel consists in their freedom from the guilt of sin, the condemning wrath of God, the rigor and curse of the Law;[1] and in their being delivered from this present evil world, bondage to Satan, and dominion of sin;[2] from the evil of afflictions, the fear and sting of death, the victory of the grave, and everlasting damnation;[3] as also in their free access to God and their yielding obedience unto Him, not out of a slavish fear, but a child-like love and willing mind.[4]

All which were common also to believers under the Law for the substance of them,[5] but under the New Testament, the liberty of Christians is further enlarged in their freedom from the yoke of the ceremonial law, to which the Jewish church was subjected, and in greater boldness of access to the throne of grace, and in fuller communications of the free Spirit of God than believers under the Law did ordinarily partake of.[6]

[1] John 3:3; Rom. 8:33; Gal. 3:13
[2] Acts 26:18; Rom. 6:14-18; 8:3; Gal. 1:4; Eph. 2:1-3; Col. 1:13
[3] Rom. 8:28; 1 Cor. 15:54-57; 1 Thess. 1:10; 2 Thess. 1:10; Heb. 2:14-15
[4] Luke 1:73-75; Rom. 8:15; Eph. 2:18; 3:12; 1 John 4:18
[5] Ps. 19:7-9; 119:14, 24, 45, 47, 48, 72, 97; John 8:32; Rom. 4:5-11; Gal. 3:9, 14; Heb. 11:27, 33-34
[6] John 1:17; 7:38-39; Gal. 2:11f.; 4:1-3; Col. 2:16-17; Heb. 1:1-2a; 7:19, 22; 8:6; 9:23; 10:19-21; 11:40

ARTICLE 2

God alone is Lord of the conscience[7] and has left it free
from the doctrines and commandments of men, which
are in anything contrary to His Word or not contained
in it.[8] So that to believe such doctrines or obey such
commands out of conscience[9] is to betray true liberty of
conscience[10] and the requiring of an implicit faith and
absolute and blind obedience is to destroy liberty of
conscience and reason also.[15]

God alone is
Lord of the
conscience...

[7] Rom. 14:4; Gal. 5:1; Jas. 4:12
[8] Matt. 15:9; Acts 4:19, 29; 5:29; 1 Cor. 7:23
[9] Gal. 1:10; 2:3-5; 5:1; Col. 2:20, 22-23
[10] John 4:22; Acts 17:11; Rom. 10:17; 14:23; 1 Cor. 3:5; 2
Cor. 1:24

ARTICLE 3

They who upon pretense of Christian liberty do practice
any sin or cherish any sinful lust, as they do thereby
pervert the main design of the grace of the Gospel to
their own destruction,[11] so they wholly destroy the end
of Christian liberty, which is, that being delivered out of
the hands of all our enemies, we might serve the Lord
without fear, in holiness and righteousness before Him,
all the days of our life.[12]

[11] Rom. 6:1-2
[12] Luke 1:74-75; Rom. 14:9; Gal. 5:13; 2 Pet. 2:18, 21

Chapter 22

Of Religious Worship and the Sabbath Day

But the Sabbath is God's merciful appointment for the common benefit of all mankind. It was "made for man" (Mark 2:27). It was given for the good of all classes, for the laity quite as much as for the clergy. It is not a yoke, but a blessing. It is not a burden, but a mercy. It is not a hard wearisome requirement, but a mighty public benefit. It is not an ordinance which man is bid to use in faith, without knowing why he uses it. It is one which carries with it its own reward. It is good for man's body and mind. It is good for nations.
Above all, it is good for souls.[y]
– J. C. Ryle

Chapter 22

The light of
nature shows
that there is a
God, who has
lordship and
sovereignty
over all...

ARTICLE 1

The light of nature shows that there is a God, who has lordship and sovereignty over all, is just, good, and does good unto all; and is therefore to be feared, loved, praised, called upon, trusted in, and served with all the heart and all the soul and with all the might.[1] But the acceptable way of worshipping the true God is instituted by Himself and so limited by His own revealed Will that He may not be worshipped according to the imaginations and devices of men or the suggestions of Satan under any visible representations or any other way not prescribed in the Holy Scriptures.[2]

[1] Jer. 10:7; Mark 12:33
[2] Gen. 4:1-5; Exo. 20:4-6; Lev. 10:1-3; Deut. 4:2; 12:29-32; 17:3; Josh. 1:7; 23:6-8; 2 Kgs. 16:10-18; Matt. 15:3, 8-9; 15:13; Col. 2:20-23; 2 Tim. 3:15-17

ARTICLE 2

Religious worship is to be given to God the Father, Son, and Holy Spirit and to Him alone;[3] not to angels, saints, or any other creatures;[4] and since the Fall, not without a mediator nor in the mediation of any other but Christ alone.[5]

[3] Matt. 4:9-10; 28:19; John 4:23; 5:23; 2 Cor. 13:14
[4] Rom. 1:25; Col. 2:10, 18; Rev. 19:10
[5] John 14:6; Eph. 2:18; Col. 3:17; 1 Tim. 2:5

ARTICLE 3

Prayer with thanksgiving, being one special part of natural worship, is by God required of all men.[6] But that it may be accepted, it is to be made in the name of the Son,[7] by the help of the Spirit,[8] according to His will;[9] with understanding, reverence, humility, fervency, faith, love, and perseverance;[10] and when with others, in a known tongue.[11]

[6] Ps. 65:2; 95:1-7; 100:1-5
[7] John 14:13-14
[8] Rom. 8:26
[9] 1 John 5:14
[10] Gen. 18:27; Ps. 47:7; Eccl. 5:1-2; Matt. 6:12, 14-15; Mark 11:24; Eph. 6:18; Col. 4:2; Heb. 12:28; Jas. 5:16; 1:6-7
[11] 1 Cor. 14:13-19, 27-28

ARTICLE 4

Prayer is to be made for things lawful and for all sorts of men living or that shall live hereafter;[12] but not for the dead nor for those of whom it may be known that they have sinned the sin unto death.[13]

[12] 2 Sam. 7:29; John 5:14; 17:20; 1 Tim. 2:1-2
[13] 2 Sam. 12:21-23; Luke 16:25-26; 1 John 5:16; Rev. 14:13

ARTICLE 5

The reading of the Scriptures,[14] preaching, and hearing the Word of God,[15] teaching and admonishing one another in psalms, hymns, and spiritual songs, singing with grace in our hearts to the Lord,[15] as also the administration of baptism[17] and the Lord's Supper[18] are all parts of religious worship of God to be performed in obedience to Him with understanding, faith, reverence, and godly fear; moreover solemn humiliation[19] with

...in the name of the Son, by the help of the Spirit, according to His will...

133

fastings[20] and thanksgiving upon special occasions ought to be used in an holy and religious manner.[21]

[14] Acts 15:21; 1 Tim. 4:13; Rev. 1:3
[15] Luke 8:18; 2 Tim. 4:2
[16] Eph. 5:19; Col. 3:16
[17] Matt. 28:19-20
[18] 1 Cor. 11:26
[19] Esth. 4:16; Joel. 2:12; Matt. 9:15; Acts 13:2-3; 1 Cor. 7:5
[20] Esth. 4:16; Joel. 2:12
[21] Exo. 15:1-19, Ps. 107

ARTICLE 6

Neither prayer nor any other part of religious worship is now under the Gospel tied unto or made more acceptable by any place in which it is performed or towards which it is directed,[22] but God is to be worshipped everywhere in Spirit and in truth;[23] as in private families[24] daily[25] and in secret each one by himself,[26] so more solemnly in the public assemblies,[27] which are not carelessly nor willfully to be neglected or forsaken, when God by His Word or providence calls thereunto.[28]

...God is to be worshipped everywhere in Spirit and in truth...

[22] John 4:21
[23] John 4:21, 23-24; Mal. 1:11; 1 Tim. 2:8
[24] Deut. 6:6-7; Job 1:5; Acts 10:2; 1 Pet. 3:7
[25] Ps. 55:17; Matt. 6:11
[26] Matt. 6:6
[27] Ps. 84:1-2, 10; Matt. 18:20; 1 Cor. 3:16; 14:25; Eph. 2:21-22
[28] Acts 2:42; Heb. 10:25

ARTICLE 7

As it is of the law of nature that in general a proportion of time by God's appointment be set apart for the worship of God, so by His Word, in a positive moral and perpetual commandment binding all men in all ages, He has particularly appointed one day in seven for a sabbath to be kept holy unto Him,[29] which from the beginning of the world to the resurrection of Christ was the last day of the week; and from the resurrection of Christ was changed into the first day of the week which is called the Lord's Day;[30] and is to be continued to the end of the world as the Christian Sabbath; the observation of the last day of the week being abolished.[31]

[29] Gen. 2:3; Exo. 20:8-11; Mark 2:27-28; Rev. 1:10
[30] Acts 20:7; 1 Cor. 16:1-2; Rev. 1:10
[31] John 10:21; Acts 2:1; 20:7; 1 Cor. 16:1; Col. 2:16-17; Rev. 1:10

ARTICLE 8

The Sabbath is then kept holy unto the Lord, when men after a due preparing of their hearts and ordering their common affairs aforehand, do not only observe an holy rest all the day from their own works, words, and thoughts[32] about their worldly employment and recreations,[33] but also are taken up the whole time in the public and private exercises of His worship and in the duties of necessity and mercy.[34]

...the whole time in the public and private exercises of His worship and in the duties of necessity and mercy.

[32] Exo. 20:8-11; Neh. 13:15-22; Isa. 58:13-14; Rev. 1:10
[33] Neh. 13:15-22; Isa. 58:13
[34] Matt. 12:1-13; Mark 2:27-28

Chapter 23

Of Lawful Oaths and Vows

When thou speakest, let thy word be as authentic as thy oath. Imitate God, who is the pattern of truth. Pythagoras being asked what made men like God, answered,...'when they speak the truth.' The character of a man that shall go to heaven, is that 'He speaketh the truth in his heart.' Psa xv 2.ᶻ
– Thomas Watson

Chapter 23

ARTICLE 1

A lawful oath is a part of religious worship, wherein the person swearing in truth, righteousness, and judgment solemnly calls God to witness what he swears[1] and to judge him according to the truth or falseness thereof.[2]

[1] Exo. 20:7; Deut. 10:20; Jer. 4:2
[2] Exo. 20:7; Lev. 19:12; Deut. 10:20; 2 Chr. 6:22-23; 2 Cor. 1:23

ARTICLE 2

The name of God only is that by which men ought to swear and therein it is to be used with all holy fear and reverence; therefore to swear vainly or rashly by that glorious and dreadful name or to swear at all by any other thing is sinful and to be abhorred;[3] yet as in matter of weight and moment for confirmation of truth and ending all strife, an oath is warranted by the Word of God; so a lawful oath being imposed by lawful authority in such matters ought to be taken.[4]

[3] Exo. 20:7; Deut. 6:13; Jer. 5:7; Matt. 5:34, 37; Jas. 5:12
[4] Gen. 24:3; 47:30-32; 50:25; Exo. 22:11; Num. 5:19, 21;
1 Kgs. 8:31; 17:1; Ezra 10:5; Neh. 5:12; 13:25; Isa. 45:23;
65:16; Matt. 26:62-64; Acts 18:18; Rom. 1:9; 2 Cor. 1:23;
Heb. 6:13-16

ARTICLE 3

Whosoever takes an oath warranted by the Word of God ought duly to consider the weightiness of so solemn an act and therein to avouch nothing but what he knows to be the truth; for that by rash, false, and vain oaths, the Lord is provoked and for them this land mourns.[5]

[5] Exo. 20:7; Lev. 19:12; Num. 30:2; Jer. 4:2; 23:10

ARTICLE 4

An oath is to be taken in the plain and common sense of the words without equivocation or mental reservation.[6]

[6] Ps. 24:4; Jer. 4:2

ARTICLE 5

A vow, which is not to be made to any creature but to God alone,[7] is to be made and performed with all religious care and faithfulness;[8] but popish monastical vows of perpetual single life, professed poverty,[9] and regular obedience are so far from being degrees of higher perfection that they are superstitious and sinful snares in which no Christian may entangle himself.[10]

...is to be made and performed with all religious care...

[7] Num. 30:2-3; Ps. 76:11; Jer. 44:25-26
[8] Gen. 28:20-22; Num. 30:2; Ps 61:8; 66:13-14; 76:11; Eccl. 5:4-6; Isa. 19:21; 1 Cor. 7:2, 9
[9] Eph. 4:28
[10] Matt. 19:11-12; 1 Cor. 6:18 with 7:2, 9; 7:23; Eph. 4:28; 1 Tim. 4:3

Chapter 24

Of the Civil Magistrate

*We acknowledge and affirm, that magistracy and civil government in
empires, kingdoms, dominions, and cities, is an ordinance of God for
his own glory, and for the great good of mankind, so that whoever are
enemies to magistracy, they are enemies to mankind,
and to the revealed will of God.[aa]*
– George Gillespie

Chapter 24

ARTICLE 1

God the supreme Lord and King of all the world has ordained civil magistrates to be under Him...

God the supreme Lord and King of all the world has ordained civil magistrates to be under Him, over the people[1] for His own glory and the public good[2] and to this end has armed them with the power of the sword for defense and encouragement of them that do good and for the punishment of evildoers.[3]

[1] Ps. 82:1; Luke 12:48; Rom. 13:1-6; 1 Pet. 2:13-14
[2] Gen. 6:11-13; 9:5-6; Ps. 58:1-2; 72:14; 82:1-4; Pro. 21:15; 24:11-12; 29:14, 26; 31:5; Ezek. 7:23; 45:9; Dan. 4:27; Matt. 22:21; Rom. 13:3-4; 1 Tim. 2:2; 1 Pet. 2:14
[3] Gen. 9:6; Pro. 16:14; 19:12; 20:2; 21:15; 28:17; Acts 25:11; Rom. 13:1-4; 1 Pet. 2:14

ARTICLE 2

It is lawful for Christians to accept and execute the office of a magistrate when called thereunto;[4] in the management whereof, as they ought especially to maintain justice and peace[5] according to the wholesome laws of each kingdom and commonwealth, so for that end, they may lawfully now under the New Testament wage war upon just and necessary occasions.[6]

[4] Exo. 22:8-9, 28-29; Daniel; Nehemiah; Pro. 14:35; 16:10, 12; 20:26, 28; 25:2; 28:15-16; 29:4, 14; 31:4-5; Rom. 13:2, 4, 6
[5] 2 Sam. 23:3; Ps. 82:3-4
[6] Luke 3:14; Rom. 13:4

ARTICLE 3

Civil magistrates being set up by God for the ends aforesaid, subjection[7] in all lawful things[8] commanded by them ought to be yielded by us in the Lord, not only for wrath but for conscience sake;[9] and we ought to make supplications and prayers for kings and all that are in authority, that, under them, we may live a quiet and peaceable life in all godliness and honesty.[10]

[7] Pro. 16:14-15; 19:12; 20:2; 24:21-22; 25:15; 28:2; Rom. 13:1-7; Tit. 3:1; 1 Pet. 2:13-14

[8] Dan. 1:8; 3:4-6, 16-18; 6:5-10, 22; Matt. 22:21; Acts 4:19-20; 5:29

[9] Rom. 13:5-7; 1 Pet. 2:17

[10] Jer. 29:7; 1 Tim. 2:1-4

...we ought to make supplications and prayers for kings and all that are in authority...

Chapter 25

Of Marriage

*The love of Christ to the church is proposed as an example of this,
which love of his is a sincere, a pure, an ardent, and constant affection,
and that notwithstanding the imperfections and failures that she is
guilty of. The greatness of his love to the church appeared in his giving
himself unto the death for it. Observe, As the church's subjection
to Christ is proposed as an exemplar to wives, so the love of Christ
to his church is proposed as a pattern to husbands; and while such
exemplars are offered to both, and so much is required of each, neither
has reason to complain of the divine injunctions.[bb]*
– Matthew Henry

Chapter 25

Marriage is to
be between
one man and
one woman...

ARTICLE 1

Marriage is to be between one man and one woman; neither is it lawful for any man to have more than one wife nor for any woman to have more than one husband at the same time.[1]

[1] Gen. 2:24; Mal. 2:15; Matt. 19:5-6; 1 Tim. 3:2; Tit. 1:6

ARTICLE 2

Marriage was ordained for the mutual help of husband and wife[2] for the increase of mankind with a legitimate issue[3] and for preventing of uncleanness.[4]

[2] Gen. 2:18; Pro. 2:17; Mal. 2:14
[3] Gen. 1:28; Ps. 127:3-5; 128:3-4
[4] 1 Cor. 7:2, 9

ARTICLE 3

It is lawful for all sorts of people to marry who are able with judgment to give their consent;[5] yet it is the duty of Christians to marry in the Lord and therefore such as profess the true religion should not marry with infidels or idolaters; neither should such as are godly be unequally yoked by marrying with such as are wicked in their life or maintain damnable heresy.[6]

[5] 1 Cor. 7:39; 2 Cor. 6:14; 1 Tim. 4:3; Heb. 13:4
[6] Neh. 13:25-27; 1 Cor. 7:39; 2 Cor. 6:14

ARTICLE 4

Marriage ought not to be within the degrees of consanguinity or affinity forbidden in the Word,[7] nor can such incestuous marriage ever be made lawful by any law of man or consent of parties so as those persons may live together as man and wife.[8]

[7] Lev. 18
[8] Lev. 18:6-18; Amos 2:7; Mark 6:18; 1 Cor. 5:1

Chapter 26

Of the Church

The Members of the Church have all One Head, the Redeemer, Saviour, Mediator, Jesus Christ, Ephes. 4. 5. As the Commonwealth is denominated from the Unity of the Sovereign Power that Heads it; so the Church is hence principally denominated One from Christ, who is the Head, the Sovereign, and the Center of it. And therefore it is called frequently his Body, and he the Head of it...He is the Foundation, and the Church is the Building that is erected upon him, and other Foundation can no Man lay, I Cor. 3. 11, 12. From this Head the whole Body fitly joined together, and compacted by that which every Joint supplieth, according to the effectual working of the Measure of every Part, maketh Increase of the Body to the Edifying of itself in Love, Ephes. 4. 16. All therefore are Members of the Catholic Church that are Members of Christ.[cc]
– Richard Baxter

Chapter 26

ARTICLE 1

The catholic or universal church,[1] which (with respect to the internal work of the Spirit and truth of grace) may be called invisible, consists of the whole number of the elect that have been, are, or shall be gathered into one under Christ the Head thereof, and is the spouse, the body, the fullness of Him that fills all in all.[2]

[1] Matt. 6:18; 1 Cor. 12:28; Eph. 1:22; 4:11-15; 5:23-25, 27, 29, 32; Col. 1:18, 24; Heb. 12:23
[2] Eph. 1:10, 22-23; 4:11-15; 5:23-25, 27, 29, 32; Col. 1:18, 24; Heb. 12:23; Rev. 21:9-14

ARTICLE 2

All persons throughout the world professing the faith of the Gospel and obedience unto God by Christ according unto it, not destroying their own profession by any errors everting the foundation or unholiness of conversation, are and may be called visible saints;[2] and of such ought all particular congregations to be constituted.[3]

[2] Matt. 16:18; 28:15-20; Acts 11:26; Rom. 1:7-8; 1 Cor. 1:2; 5:1-9
[3] Matt. 18:15-20; Acts 2:37-42; 4:4; Rom. 1:7; 1 Cor. 5:1-9; Eph. 1:20-22

ARTICLE 3

The purest churches under heaven are subject to mixture and error...

The purest churches under heaven are subject to mixture and error,[4] and some have so degenerated as to become no churches of Christ but synagogues of Satan;[5] nevertheless Christ always has had and ever shall have a kingdom in this world to the end thereof of such as believe in Him and make profession of His name.[6]

[4] 1 Cor. 1:11; 5; 6:6; 11:17-19; 3 John 9-10; Rev. 2 and 3
[5] 2 Thess. 2:11-12; 1 Tim. 3:14-15; Rev. 1:20; 2:5; 18:2
[6] Matt. 16:18; 24:14; 28:20; Mark 4:30-32; Ps. 72:16-18; 102:28; Isa. 9:6-7; Rev. 12:17; 20:7-9

ARTICLE 4

The Lord Jesus Christ is the Head of the Church, in whom, by the appointment of the Father,[7] all power for the calling, institution, order, or government of the Church is invested in a supreme and sovereign manner;[7] neither can the Pope of Rome in any sense be head thereof, but is that Antichrist, that man of sin and son of perdition, that exalts himself in the Church against Christ and all that is called God, whom the Lord shall destroy with the brightness of His coming.[8]

The Lord Jesus Christ is the Head of the Church...

[7] Matt. 28:18-20; John 10:14-16; 17:1-3; Acts 5:31; 1 Cor. 12:27-28; Eph. 4:11-16; 1:20-23; 5:23-32; Col. 1:18
[8] 2 Thess. 2:2-9

ARTICLE 5

In the execution of this power wherewith He is so entrusted, the Lord Jesus calls out of the world unto Himself, through the ministry of His Word by His Spirit, those that are given unto Him by His Father,[9] that they may walk before Him in all the ways of obedience, which He prescribes to them in His Word.[10] Those thus called, He commands to walk together in particular societies or churches for their mutual edification and the due performance of that public worship, which He requires of them in the world.[11]

[9] John 10:16, 23; 12:32; 17:2; Acts 5:31-32
[10] Matt. 28:20
[11] Matt. 18:15-20; Acts 14:21-23; 1 Tim 1:3; 3:14-16; 5:17-22; Tit. 1:5

ARTICLE 6

The members of these churches are saints by calling...

The members of these churches are saints by calling, visibly manifesting and evidencing (in and by their profession and walking) their obedience unto that call of Christ,[12] and do willingly consent to walk together according to the appointment of Christ, giving up themselves to the Lord and one to another by the will of God, in professed subjection to the ordinances of the Gospel.[13]

[12] Matt. 28:18-20; Acts 2:37-42; 4:4; 5:13-14; 14:22-23; Rom. 1:7; 1 Cor. 1:2, 13-17; 1 Thess. 1:1, 2-10
[13] Acts 2:41-42; 5:13-14; 2 Cor. 9:13

ARTICLE 7

To each of these churches thus gathered, according to His mind declared in His Word, He has given all that power and authority, which is any way needful for their carrying on that order in worship and discipline which He has instituted for them to observe, with commands and rules for the due and right exerting and executing of that power.[14]

[14] Matt. 18:17-20; 1 Cor. 5:4-5, 13; 2 Cor. 2:6-8

ARTICLE 8

A particular church gathered and completely organized according to the mind of Christ consists of officers and members; and the officers appointed by Christ to be chosen and set apart by the church (so called and gathered) for the peculiar administration of ordinances and execution of power or duty, which He entrusts them with or calls them to, to be continued to the end of the world are bishops or elders and deacons.[15]

[15] Acts 20:17, 28; Phil. 1:1; 1 Tim. 3:1-13; Tit. 1:5-7; 1 Pet. 5:2

ARTICLE 9

The way appointed by Christ for the calling of any person, fitted and gifted by the Holy Spirit[16] unto the office of bishop or elder in a church, is that he be chosen thereunto by the common suffrage of the church itself[17] and solemnly set apart by fasting and prayer with imposition of hands of the eldership of the church, if there be any before constituted therein;[18] and of a deacon that he be chosen by the like suffrage and set apart by prayer and the like imposition of hands.[19]

[16] Eph. 4:11; 1 Tim. 3:1-13
[17] Matt. 18:17-20; Acts 6:1-7; 14:23; 1 Cor. 5:1-13
[18] 1 Tim. 4:14; 5:22
[19] Acts 6:1-7

ARTICLE 10

The work of pastors being constantly to attend the service of Christ in His churches, in the ministry of the Word and prayer, with watching for their souls as they that must give an account to Him;[20] it is incumbent on the churches to whom they minister not only to give them all due respect but also to communicate to them

The work of pastors being constantly to attend the service of Christ...

...so as they
may have a
comfortable
supply
without being
themselves
entangled
in secular
affairs...

of all their good things according to their ability,[21] so
as they may have a comfortable supply without being
themselves entangled in secular affairs;[22] and may also be
capable of exercising hospitality toward others;[23] and this
is required by the law of nature and by the express order
of our Lord Jesus, who has ordained that they that preach
the Gospel should live of the Gospel.[24]

[20] Acts 6:4; 1 Tim. 3:2; 5:17; Heb. 13:17
[21] 1 Cor. 9:14; Gal. 6:6-7; 1 Tim. 5:17-18
[22] 2 Tim. 2:4
[23] 1 Tim. 3:2
[24] 1 Cor. 9:6-14; 1 Tim. 5:8

ARTICLE 11

Although it be incumbent on the bishops or pastors of
the churches to be instant in preaching the Word by way
of office, yet the work of preaching the Word is not so
peculiarly confined to them but that others also gifted
and fitted by the Holy Spirit for it and approved and
called by the Church may and ought to perform it.[25]

[25] Acts 8:5; 11:19-21; 1 Pet. 4:10-11

ARTICLE 12

As all believers are bound to join themselves to particular
churches when and where they have opportunity so
to do, so all that are admitted unto the privileges of a
Church are also[24] under the censures and government
thereof, according to the rule of Christ.[26]

[26] 1 Cor. 5:9-13; 1 Thess. 5:14; 2 Thess. 3:6, 14-15; Heb.
13:17

ARTICLE 13

No church members upon any offense taken by them, having performed their duty required of them towards the person they are offended at, ought to disturb any church order or absent themselves from the assemblies of the church or administration of any ordinances upon the account of such offense at any of their fellow members; but to wait upon Christ in the further proceeding of the church.[27]

... but to wait upon Christ in the further proceeding of the church.

[27] Matt. 18:15-17; 28:20; Eph. 4:2-3; Col. 3:12-15; 1 John 2:7-11, 18-19; 28:15-17

ARTICLE 14

As each church and all the members of it are bound to pray continually for the good and prosperity of all the churches of Christ in all places and upon all occasions to further it (every one within the bounds of their places and callings in the exercise of their gifts and graces),[28] so the churches (when planted by the providence of God so as they may enjoy opportunity and advantage for it)[29] ought to hold communion amongst themselves for their peace, increase of love, and mutual edification.[30]

[28] Ps. 122:6; John 13:34-35; 17:11, 21-23; Rom. 16:1-3; 15:26; 2 Cor. 8:1-4, 16-24; 9:12-15; Eph. 4:11-16; 6:18; Col. 1:3, 4, 7; 2:1; 4:7, 12; 2 John 5-11; 3 John 8-10
[29] Rom. 16:1-2; Gal. 1:2, 22; Col. 4:16; 3 John 8-10; Rev. 1:4
[30] Josh. 22; Rom. 16:1-3; 2 Cor. 9:12-15; 1 John 4:1-3; 2 John; 3 John

Chapter 26

ARTICLE 15

In cases of difficulties or differences, either in point of doctrine or administration wherein either the churches in general are concerned, or any one church in their peace, union, and edification, or any member or members of any church are injured in or by any proceedings in censures not agreeable to truth and order, it is according to the mind of Christ that many churches holding communion together do by their messengers meet to consider and give their advice in or about that matter in difference to be reported to all the churches concerned;[31] howbeit these messengers assembled are not entrusted with any church power properly so called or with any jurisdiction over the churches themselves to exercise any censures either over any churches or persons or to impose their determination on the churches or officers.[32]

...howbeit these messengers assembled are not entrusted with any church power properly so called...

[31] Pro. 3:5-7; 12:15; 13:10; Acts 15:2, 4, 6, 22-23, 25; Gal. 2:2

[32] 1 Cor. 7:25, 36, 40; 2 Cor. 1:24; 1 John 4:1

Chapter 27

Of the Communion of Saints

But this is the order of the communion of saints. The foundation of it is laid in a join participation of the same quickening Spirit, and union with Christ thereby. It is acted and exercised by love arising from this spring; and it is expressed in our joint participation of the same ordinances of worship. Hence it is apparent that where this love is not, there is no communion of saints, nor any thing belonging thereto. For our participation together in the same ordinances is no part thereof, unless the influence of our original communion in the participation of the same Spirit be conveyed thereunto by love,
by which alone it is acted.[dd]
– John Owen

Chapter 27

ARTICLE 1

All saints that are united to Jesus Christ,[1] their Head by His Spirit and faith[2] (although they are not made thereby one person with Him),[3] have fellowship in His graces, sufferings, death, resurrection, and glory;[4] and being united to one another in love, they have communion in each others gifts and graces[5] and are obliged to the performance of such duties, public and private, in an orderly way, as do conduce to their mutual good, both in the inward and outward man.[6]

[1] John 17:2, 6; Rom. 6:8; 8:17; 8:2; 1 Cor. 6:17; 2 Cor. 5:21; Eph. 1:4; 2 Pet. 1:4
[2] 2 Cor. 3:17-18; Gal. 2:20; Eph. 3:16-17
[3] Ps. 45:7; Isa. 42:8; 1 Cor. 8:6; Col. 1:18-19; 1 Tim. 6:15-16; Heb. 1:8-9
[4] John 1:16; 15:1-6; Rom. 4:25; 6:1-6; Eph. 2:4-6; Phil. 3:10; Col. 3:3-4; 1 John 1:3;
[5] John 13:34-35; 14:15; Rom. 14:7-8; 1 Cor. 3:21-23; 12:7, 25-27; Eph. 4:15-16; 1 Pet. 4:10
[6] Rom. 1:12; 12:10-13; Gal. 6:10; Col. 6:10; 1 Thess. 5:11, 14; 1 John 3:17-18; 1 Pet. 3:8

ARTICLE 2

Saints by profession are bound to maintain an holy fellowship and communion in the worship of God and in performing such other spiritual services as tend to their mutual edification;[7] as also in relieving each other in outward things according to their several abilities and necessities;[8] which communion according to the rule of the Gospel, though especially to be exercised by them in the relations wherein they stand, whether in families[9] or churches,[10] yet as God offers opportunity is to be extended to all the household of faith, even all those who in every place call upon the name of the Lord Jesus;[11] nevertheless their communion one with another as saints does not take away or infringe the title or propriety which each man has in his goods and possessions.[12]

[7] Heb. 3:12-13; 10:24-25
[8] Acts 11:29-30; Rom. 15; 2 Cor. 8-9; Gal. 2
[9] Eph. 6:4
[10] 1 Cor. 12:14-27; Eph. 6:4; 1 Tim. 5:8, 16
[11] Acts 11:29-30; Rom. 15; 2 Cor. 8-9; Gal. 2; 6:10
[12] Exo. 20:15; Acts 5:4; Eph. 4:28

...does not take away or infringe the title or propriety which each man has in his goods and possessions.

Chapter 28

Of Baptism and the Lord's Supper

A sacrament ought to be a testimony of the good-will of God toward us. Of this no man or angel can be witness, since God has no counsellor, (Isa. xl. 13; Rom. xi. 34.) He himself alone, with legitimate authority, testifies of himself to us by his word. A sacrament is a seal of attestation or promise of God. Now, it could not be sealed by corporeal things, or the elements of this world, unless they were confirmed and set apart for this purpose by the will of God. Man, therefore, cannot institute a sacrament, because it is not in the power of man to make such divine mysteries lurk under things so abject. The word of God must precede to make a sacrament to be a sacrament, as Augustine most admirably shows (Hom. in Joann. 80.)[ee]
– John Calvin

Chapter 28

...appointed
by the Lord
Jesus the only
Lawgiver...

ARTICLE 1

Baptism and the Lord's Supper are ordinances of positive and sovereign institution, appointed by the Lord Jesus the only Lawgiver,[1] to be continued in His Church to the end of the world.[2]

[1] Matt. 28:19-20; 1 Cor. 11:24-25
[2] Matt. 28:18-20; Luke 22:14-20; Rom. 6:3-4; 1 Cor. 1:13-17; 11:26; Gal. 3:27; Eph. 4:5; Col. 2:12; 1 Pet. 3:21

ARTICLE 2

These holy appointments are to be administered by those only who are qualified and thereunto called according to the commission of Christ.[3]

[3] Matt. 24:45-51; 28:19; Luke 12:41-44; 1 Cor. 4:1; Tit. 1:5-7

Chapter 29

Of Baptism

In matters of worship there ought to be a command for what is done; as this ordinance of baptism is a solemn act of worship, being performed in the name of the Father, and of the Son, and of the holy Ghost. God is a jealous God, and especially with respect to the worship of him; nor should any thing be introduced into it but what he has commanded; and careful should we be hereof, lest he should say unto us, who hath required this at your hands? it is not enough that such and such things are not forbidden; for on this footing a thousand fooleries may be brought into the worship of God, which will be resented by him.[ff]
– John Gill

ARTICLE 1

...a sign of his
fellowship
with Him in
His death and
resurrection...

Baptism is an ordinance of the New Testament ordained by Jesus Christ to be unto the party baptized a sign of his fellowship with Him in His death and resurrection, of his being engrafted into Him,[1] of remission of sins,[2] and of his giving up unto God through Jesus Christ to live and walk in newness of life.[3]

[1] Rom. 6:3-5; Gal. 3:27; Col. 2:12
[2] Mark 1:4; Acts 22:16
[3] Rom. 6:2, 4

ARTICLE 2

Those who do actually profess repentance towards God, faith in, and obedience to our Lord Jesus are the only proper subjects of this ordinance.[4]

[4] Jer. 31:31-34; Matt. 3:1-12; 21:43; 28:19-20; Mark 1:4-6; 16:15-16; Luke 3:3-6; John 1:12-13; 4:1-2; Acts 2:37-41; 8:12-13, 36-38; 9:18; 10:47-48; 11:16; 15:9; 16:14-15, 31-34; 18:8; 19:3-5; 22:16; Rom. 6:3-4; 1 Cor. 1:13-17; Gal. 3:27; Phil. 3:3; Col. 2:12; 1 Pet. 3:21

ARTICLE 3

The outward element to be used in this ordinance is water, wherein the party is to be baptized[5] in the name of the Father and of the Son and of the Holy Spirit.[6]

[5] Matt. 3:11; Acts 8:36, 38; 22:16
[6] Matt. 28:18-20; Acts 8:38

ARTICLE 4

Immersion or dipping of the person in water is necessary to the due administration of this ordinance.[7]

[7] 2 Kgs. 5:14; Ps. 69:2; Isa. 21:4; Matt. 3:11, 16; Mark 1:5, 8-9; 7:3-4; 10:38-39; Luke 12:50; John 3:23; Acts 1:5, 8; 2:1-4, 17; 8:38; Rom. 6:4; 1 Cor. 10:1-2; Col. 2:12

Immersion or dipping of the person in water is necessary...

Chapter 30

Of the Lord's Supper

The great object of the your thoughts is however, the Master of the feast, the Lord Jesus, here 'evidently set forth crucified' (Gal. 3:1). When he is vividly before your mind, in his agonies and death, believe on him, rest in him, cleave to him. By faith feed on him, as 'the Bread of life' (John 6:48, 51, 53, 56). Do not hesitate to let the full tide of your affections flow out to him. Love him, as infinitely holy and gracious. 'Set to your seal that God is true' (John 3:33) and appropriate him as yours; saying, 'My Lord, and my God!' (John 20:28). Adore the ineffable glory of God as it shines in the fact of Jesus Christ. And renew your covenant, by yielding yourself irrevocably to him, as your Lord and King. These are but examples of the acts of a happy soul in communion with Christ at his Table.[gg]
– J. W. Alexander

Chapter 30

ARTICLE 1

The supper of the Lord Jesus was instituted by Him the same night wherein He was betrayed[1] to be observed in His churches[2] unto the end of the world[3] for the perpetual remembrance and showing forth the sacrifice of Himself in His death,[4] confirmation of the faith of believers in all the benefits thereof,[5] their spiritual nourishment and growth in Him,[6] their further engagement in and to all duties which they owe unto Him,[7] and to be a bond and pledge of their communion with Him and with each other.[8]

[1] Matt. 26:20-26; Mark 14:17-22; Luke 22:19-23; 1 Cor. 11:23
[2] Acts 2:41-42; 20:7; 1 Cor. 11:17-22, 33-34
[3] Mark 14:24-25; Luke 22:17-22; 1 Cor. 11:24-26
[4] Matt. 26:27-28; Luke 22:19-20; 1 Cor. 11:23-26
[5] Rom. 4:11
[6] John 6:29, 35, 47-58
[7] 1 Cor. 11:25
[8] 1 Cor. 10:16-17, 21

ARTICLE 2

In this ordinance, Christ is not offered up to His Father nor any real sacrifice made at all for remission of sin of the quick or dead, but only a memorial of that one offering up of Himself by Himself upon the cross once for all[9] and a spiritual oblation of all possible praise unto God for the same[10] so that the popish sacrifice of the mass (as they call it) is most abominable, injurious to Christ's own only sacrifice, the alone propitiation for all the sins of the elect.

[9] Luke 22:19; John 19:30; 1 Cor. 11:24-25; Heb. 9:25-28; 10:10-14
[10] Matt. 26:26-27, 30; 1 Cor. 11:24; Heb. 13:10-16

ARTICLE 3

The Lord Jesus has in this ordinance appointed His ministers to pray and bless the elements of bread and wine and thereby to set them apart from a common to an holy use and to take and break the bread, to take the cup, and (they communicating also themselves) to give both to the communicants.[11]

The Lord Jesus has... appointed...

[11] Matt. 26:26-28; Mark 14:22-25; Luke 22:19-22; 1 Cor. 11:23-26

ARTICLE 4

The denial of the cup to the people,[12] worshipping the elements, the lifting them up, or carrying them about for adoration and reserving them for any pretended religious use are all contrary to the nature of this ordinance and to the institution of Christ.[13]

[12] Matt. 26:27; Mark 14:23; 1 Cor. 11:25-28
[13] Exo. 20:4-5; Matt. 15:9; 26:26-28

ARTICLE 5

The outward elements in this ordinance, duly set apart to the uses ordained by Christ, have such relation to Him crucified as that truly, although in terms used figuratively, they are sometimes called by the name of the things they represent, to wit, the body and blood of Christ;[14] albeit

...in substance and nature, they still remain truly and only bread and wine as they were before.

in substance and nature, they still remain truly and only bread and wine as they were before.[15]

[14] Matt. 26:26-28; 1 Cor. 11:27
[15] Matt. 26:29; 1 Cor. 11:26-28

ARTICLE 6

That doctrine which maintains a change of the substance of bread and wine into the substance of Christ's body and blood (commonly called transubstantiation) by consecration of a priest or by any other way is repugnant not to Scripture alone[16] but even to common sense and reason, overthrows the nature of the ordinance, and has been and is the cause of manifold superstitions, yea of gross idolatries.[17]

[16] Gen. 17:10-11; 41:26-27; Ezek. 37:11; Matt. 26:26-29; Luke 12:1; 24:6, 36-43, 50-51; John 1:14; 20:26-29; Acts 1:9-11; 3:21; 1 Cor. 11:24-26; Rev. 1:20
[17] 1 Cor. 11:24-25

ARTICLE 7

Worthy receivers, outwardly partaking of the visible elements in this ordinance,[18] do then also inwardly by faith, really and indeed, yet not carnally and corporally but spiritually receive and feed upon Christ crucified and all the benefits of His death;[19] the body and blood of Christ being then not corporally or carnally but spiritually present to the faith of believers in that ordinance as the elements themselves are to their outward senses.[20]

[18] 1 Cor. 11:28
[19] John 6:29, 35, 47-58
[20] 1 Cor. 10:16; 11:23-26

ARTICLE 8

All ignorant and ungodly persons, as they are unfit to enjoy communion with Christ, so are they unworthy of the Lord's Table and cannot without great sin against Him, while they remain such, partake of these holy mysteries or be admitted thereunto;[21] yea, whosoever shall receive unworthily are guilty of the body and blood of the Lord, eating and drinking judgment to themselves.[22]

...whosoever shall receive unworthily are guilty of the body and blood of the Lord...

[21] Exo. 20:7, 16; Matt. 7:6; Acts 2:41-42; 20:7; 1 Cor. 5:9-13; 11:17-22, 33-34; 2 Cor. 6:14-15; Eph. 4:17-24; 5:3-9; 2 John 10
[22] Matt. 7:6; 1 Cor. 11:20-22, 27-34

Of the State of Man After Death and of the Resurrection of the Dead

It may keep your heart from shrinking back, to consider that death is necessary to fit you for the full enjoyment of God. Whether you are willing to die or not, there certainly is no other way to complete the happiness of your soul. Death must do you the kind office to remove this veil of flesh...before you can see and enjoy him fully. "While we are at home in the body, we are absent from the Lord."[hh]
– John Flavel

Chapter 31

ARTICLE 1

The bodies of men after death return to dust and see corruption,[1] but their souls (which neither die nor sleep) having an immortal subsistence, immediately return to God who gave them;[2] the souls of the righteous being then made perfect in holiness are received into paradise where they are with Christ and behold the face of God in light and glory waiting for the full redemption of their bodies;[3] and the souls of the wicked are cast into hell where they remain in torment and utter darkness reserved to the judgment of the great day.[4] Besides these two places for souls separated from their bodies, the Scripture acknowledges none.

[1] Gen. 2:17; 3:19; Acts 13:36; Rom. 5:12-21; 1 Cor. 15:22
[2] Gen. 2:7; Eccl. 12:7; Matt. 10:28; Jas. 2:26
[3] 1 Kgs. 8:27-49; Ps. 23:6; Isa. 63:15; 66:1; Luke 23:43; Acts 1:9-11; 3:21; 2 Cor. 5:1, 6-8; 12:2-4; Eph. 4:10; Phil. 1:21-23; Heb. 1:3; 4:14-15; 6:20; 8:1; 9:24; 12:23; Rev. 6:9-11; 14:13; 20:4-6
[4] Luke 16:22-26; Acts 1:25; 1 Pet. 3:19; 2 Pet. 2:9; Jude 6-7

ARTICLE 2

At the last day, such of the saints as are found alive shall not sleep but be changed,[5] and all the dead shall be raised up[6] with the selfsame bodies and none other,[7] although with different qualities,[8] which shall be united again to their souls forever.[9]

[5] 1 Cor. 15:50-53; 2 Cor. 5:1-4; 1 Thess. 4:17
[6] Dan. 12:2; John 5:28-29; Acts 24:15
[7] Job 19:26-27; John 5:28-29; 1 Cor. 15:35-38, 42-44

[8] 1 Cor. 15:42-44, 52-54
[9] Dan. 12:2; Matt. 25:46; 1 Cor. 15:42-43

ARTICLE 3

The bodies of the unjust shall by the power of Christ be raised to dishonor;[10] the bodies of the just, by His Spirit,[11] unto honor[12] and be made conformable to His own glorious body.[13]

...be made
conformable
to His own
glorious body.

[10] Dan. 12:2; John 5:28-29
[11] Rom. 8:1, 11; 1 Cor. 15:45; Gal. 6:8
[12] 1 Cor. 15:42-49
[13] John 5:28-29; Acts 24:15; Rom. 8:17, 29-30; 1 Cor. 15:20-23, 48-49; Phil. 3:21; Col. 1:18; 3:4; 1 John 3:2; Rev. 1:5

Chapter 32

Of the Last Judgment

This doctrine affords matter of great consolation to the godly. This day of judgment, which is so terrible to ungodly men, affords no ground of terror to you, but abundant ground of joy and satisfaction. For though you now meet with more affliction and trouble than most wicked men, yet on that day you shall be delivered from all afflictions, and from all trouble. If you be unjustly treated by wicked men, and abused by them, what a comfort is it to the injured, that they may appeal to God, who judgeth righteously. The Psalmist used often to comfort himself with this.[ii]
– Jonathan Edwards

Chapter 32

God has
appointed a
day wherein
He will judge
the world in
righteousness
by Jesus
Christ...

ARTICLE 1

God has appointed a day wherein He will judge the world in righteousness by Jesus Christ, to whom all power and judgment is given of the Father,[1] in which day not only the apostate angels shall be judged,[2] but likewise all persons that have lived upon the earth shall appear before the tribunal of Christ[3] to give an account of their thoughts, words, and deeds and to receive according to what they have done in the body whether good or evil.[4]

[1] John 5:22, 27; Acts 17:31
[2] 1 Cor. 6:3; Jude 6
[3] Matt. 16:27; 25:31-46; Acts 17:30-31; Rom. 2:6-16; 2 Thess. 1:5-10; 2 Pet. 3:1-13; Rev. 20:11-15
[4] Eccl. 12:14; Rom. 14:10, 12; Matt. 12:36; 25:32-46; 1 Cor. 4:5; 2 Cor. 5:10

ARTICLE 2

The end of God's appointing this day is for the manifestation of the glory of His mercy in the eternal salvation of the elect and of His justice in the eternal damnation of the reprobate, who are wicked and disobedient,[5] for then shall the righteous go into everlasting life and receive that fullness of joy and glory with everlasting reward in the presence of the Lord; but the wicked who know not God and obey not the Gospel of Jesus Christ shall be cast into eternal torments[6] and punished with everlasting destruction from the presence of the Lord and from the glory of His power.[7]

[5] Rom. 9:22-23
[6] Matt. 25:21, 34; 2 Tim. 4:8
[7] Matt. 3:12; 5:26; 13:41-42; 18:8; 24:51; 25:30, 41, 46;

Mark 9:43, 48; Luke 3:17; 2 Thess. 1:7-10; Heb. 6:2; Jude 6; Rev. 14:10-11

ARTICLE 3

As Christ would have us to be certainly persuaded that there shall be a Day of Judgment both to deter all men from sin[8] and for the greater consolation of the godly in their adversity,[9] so will He have that day unknown to men that they may shake off all carnal security and be always watchful because they know not at what hour the Lord will come[10] and may ever be prepared to say, Come Lord Jesus, come quickly,[11] Amen.

[8] 2 Cor. 5:10-11
[9] 2 Thess. 1:5-7
[10] Mark 13:35-37; Luke 12:35-40
[11] Rev. 22:20

...to deter all men from sin and for the greater consolation of the godly in their adversity...

An Appendix
—— on Baptism ——

Whosoever reads and impartially considers what we have in our forgoing confession declared may readily perceive that we do not only concenter with all other true Christians on the Word of God (revealed in the Scriptures of truth) as the foundation and rule of our faith and worship, but that we have also industriously endeavored to manifest that in the fundamental articles of Christianity we mind the same things and have therefore expressed our belief in the same words that have on the like occasion been spoken by other societies of Christians before us.

This we have done that those who are desirous to know the principles of religion which we hold and practice may take an estimate from ourselves (who jointly concur in this work) and may not be misguided, either by undue reports or by the ignorance or errors of particular persons, who going under the same name with ourselves, may give an occasion of scandalizing the truth we profess.

And although we do differ from our brethren who are paedobaptists in the subject and administration of baptism and such other circumstances as have a necessary dependence on our observance of that ordinance and do frequent our own assemblies for our mutual edification and discharge of those duties and services which we owe unto God and in His fear to each other, yet we would not be from hence misconstrued, as if the discharge of our own consciences herein, did any way disoblige or alienate our affections or conversation from any others that fear the Lord; but that we may and do as we have opportunity participate of the labors of those whom God has endued with abilities above ourselves and qualified and called to the ministry of the Word, earnestly desiring to approve ourselves to be such as follow after peace with holiness, and therefore we always keep that blessed Irenicum or healing Word of the Apostle before our eyes: "If in any thing ye be otherwise minded, God shall reveal even this unto you. Nevertheless, whereto we have already attained, let us walk by the same rule, let us mind the same thing" (Phil. 3:15-16).

Let it not therefore be judged of us (because much has been written on this subject and yet we continue this our practice different from others) that it is out of obstinacy, but rather as the truth is, that we do herein, according to the best of our understandings, worship God out of a pure mind, yielding obedience to His precept in that method which we take to be most agreeable to the Scriptures of truth and primitive practice.

It would not become us to give any such intimation as should carry a semblance that what we do in the service of God is with a doubting conscience or with any such temper of mind that we do thus for the present with a reservation that we will do otherwise hereafter upon more mature deliberation; nor have we any cause so to do, being fully persuaded that what we do is agreeable to the will of God. Yet we do heartily propose this: that if any of the servants of our Lord Jesus shall, in the spirit of meekness, attempt to convince us of any mistake either in judgment or practice, we shall diligently ponder his arguments and account him our chiefest friend that shall be an instrument to convert us from any error that is in our ways, for we cannot wittingly do anything against the truth, but all things for the truth.

And therefore we have endeavored seriously to consider what has been already offered for our satisfaction in this point, and are loath to say anymore, lest we should be esteemed desirous of renewed contests thereabout; yet forasmuch as it may justly be expected that we show some reason why we cannot acquiesce in what has been urged against us, we shall, with as much brevity as may consist with plainness, endeavor to satisfy the expectation of those that shall peruse what we now publish in this matter also.

1. As to those Christians who consent with us, *That repentance from dead works and faith towards God and our Lord Jesus Christ is required in persons to be baptized*; and do therefore supply the defect (of the infant being uncapable of making confession of either) by others who do undertake these things for it. Although we do find by church history that this has been a very ancient practice, yet considering that the same Scripture which does caution us against censuring our brother, with whom we shall all stand before the judgment seat of Christ, does also instruct us that "every one of us shall give account of himself to God" and "whatsoever is not of faith is sin" (Rom. 14:4, 10, 12, 23). Therefore we cannot for our own parts be persuaded in our own minds to build such a practice as this upon an unwritten tradition but do rather choose in all points of faith and worship to have recourse to the Holy Scriptures for the information of our judgment and regulation of our practice; being well assured that a conscientious attending thereto is the best way to prevent and rectify our defects and errors (2 Tim. 3:16-17). And if any such case happen to be debated between Christians, which is not plainly determinable by the Scriptures, we think it safest to leave such things undecided until the second coming of our Lord Jesus, as they did in the Church of old, until there should arise a priest with Urim and Thummim that might certainly inform them of the mind of God thereabout (Ezra 2:62-63).

2. As for those our Christian brethren who do ground their arguments for infant baptism upon a presumed federal holiness or church membership, we conceive they are deficient in this, that albeit this covenant holiness and membership should be, as is supposed, in reference unto the infants of believers, yet no command for infant baptism does immediately and directly result from such a quality or relation.

All instituted worship receives its sanction from the precept and is to be thereby governed in all the necessary circumstances thereof.

So it was in the covenant that God made with Abraham and his seed. The sign whereof was appropriated only to the male, notwithstanding that the female seed as well as the male were comprehended in the covenant and part of the Church of God; neither was this sign to be affixed to any male infant till he was eight days old, albeit he was within the covenant from the first moment of his life; nor could the danger of death or any other supposed necessity warrant the circumcising of him before the set time, nor was there any cause for it; the commination of being cut off from his people being only upon the neglect or contempt of the precept.

Righteous Lot was nearly related to Abraham in the flesh and contemporary with him when this covenant was made, yet inasmuch as he did not descend from his loins nor was of his household family (although he was of the same household of faith with Abraham), yet neither Lot himself nor any of his posterity (because of their descent from him) were signed with the signature of this covenant that was made with Abraham and his seed.

This may suffice to show that where there was both an express covenant and a sign thereof (such a covenant as did separate the persons with whom it was made and all their offspring from all the rest of the world as a people holy unto the Lord and did constitute them the visible Church of God, though not comprehensive of all the faithful in the world), yet the sign of this covenant was not affixed to all the persons that were within this covenant nor to any of them till the prefixt season nor to other faithful servants of God that were not of descent from Abraham. And consequently that it depends purely upon the will of the Lawgiver to determine what shall be the sign of His covenant, unto whom, at what season, and upon what terms it shall be affixed.

If our brethren do suppose baptism to be the seal of the covenant which God makes with every believer (of which the Scriptures are altogether silent), it is not our concern to contend with them herein; yet we conceive the seal of that covenant is the indwelling of the Spirit of Christ in the particular and individual persons in whom He resides and nothing else; neither do they or we suppose that baptism is in any such manner substituted in the place of circumcision as to have the same (and no other) latitude, extent, or terms than circumcision had, for that was suited only for the male children. Baptism is an ordinance suited for every believer, whether male or female, that extended to all the males that were born in Abraham's house or bought with his money equally with the males that proceeded from his own loins, but baptism is not so far extended in any true Christian church that we know of as to be administered to all the poor infidel servants that the members thereof purchase for their service and introduce into their families, nor to the children born of them in their house.

But we conceive the same parity of reasoning may hold for the ordinance of baptism as for that of circumcision (Exo. 12:49), viz. one law for the stranger as for the home born. If any desire to be admitted to all the ordinances and privileges of God's house, the door is open upon the same terms that any one person was ever admitted to all or any of those privileges that belong to the Christian Church. May all persons of right challenge the like admission.

As for that text of Scripture, Rom. 4:11: "He received the sign of circumcision, a seal of the righteousness of the faith which he had yet being uncircumcised," we conceive if the Apostle's scope in that place be duly attended to, it will appear that no argument can be taken from thence to enforce infant baptism; and forasmuch as we find a full and fair account of those words given by the learned Dr. Lightfoot (a man not to be suspected of partiality in this controversy) in his *Hor. Hebrai* on the I Cor. 7:19, p. 42-43., we shall transcribe his words at large without any comment of our own upon them.

> *Circumcision is nothing, if we respect the time, for now it was without use, that end of it being especially fulfilled; for which it had been instituted: this end the Apostle declares in these words, Rom. 4:11 σφραγῖδα. But I fear that by most translations they are not sufficiently suited to the end of circumcision, and the scope of the Apostle whilst something of their own is by them inserted.*

And after the Doctor has represented diverse versions of the words agreeing for the most part in sense with that which we have in our Bibles, he thus proceeds:

> *Other versions are to the same purpose; as if circumcision was given to Abraham for a seal of that righteousness which he had being yet uncircumcised, which we will not deny to*

*be in some sense true, but we believe that circumcision had
chiefly a far different respect.*

*Give me leave thus to render the words; And he received the
sign of circumcision, a seal of the righteousness of faith, which
was to be in the uncircumcision, which was to be (I say) not
which had been, not that which Abraham had whilst he was
yet uncircumcised; but that which his uncircumcised seed
should have, that is the Gentiles, who in time to come should
imitate the faith of Abraham.*

*Now consider well on what occasion circumcision was
instituted unto Abraham, setting before thine eyes the history
thereof, Gen. 17.*

*This promise is first made unto him, Thou shalt be the father
of many nations (in what sense the Apostle explains in that
chapter) and then there is subjoined a double seal for the
confirmation of the thing, to wit, the change of the name
Abram into Abraham and the institution of circumcision. v.4.
Behold as for me, my covenant is with thee, and thou shalt be
the father of many nations. Wherefore was his name called
Abraham? for the sealing of this promise. Thou shalt be the
Father of many Nations. And wherefore was circumcision
instituted to him? For the sealing of the same promise.
Thou shalt be the Father of many Nations. So that this is
the sense of the Apostle; most agreeable to the institution
of circumcision; he received the sign of circumcision, a
seal of the righteousness of faith which in time to come the
uncircumcision (or the gentiles) should have and obtain.*

*Abraham had a twofold seed: natural, of the Jews; and
faithful, of the believing Gentiles: his natural seed was*

signed with the sign of circumcision, first indeed for the
distinguishing of them from all other nations whilst they
as yet were not the seed of Abraham, but especially for the
memorial of the justification of the Gentiles by faith, when at
length they should become his seed. Therefore circumcision
was of right to cease, when the Gentiles were brought into
the faith, forasmuch as then it had obtained its last and chief
end, and thenceforth circumcision is nothing.

Thus far he, which we earnestly desire may be seriously weighed, for we plead not his authority, but the evidence of truth in his words.

3. Of whatsoever nature the holiness of the children mentioned (1 Cor. 7:12) be, yet they who do conclude that all such children (whether infants or of riper years) have from hence an immediate right to baptism do, as we conceive, put more into the conclusion than will be found in the premises.

For although we do not determine positively concerning the Apostle's scope in the holiness here mentioned so as to say it is this or that and no other thing, yet it is evident that the Apostle does by it determine not only the lawfulness but the expedience also of a believer's cohabitation with an unbeliever in the state of marriage.

And we do think that although the Apostle's asserting of the unbelieving yokefellow to be sanctified by the believer should carry in it somewhat more than is in the bare marriage of two infidels, because although the marriage covenant have a Divine sanction so as to make the wedlock of two unbelievers a lawful action and their conjunction and cohabitation in that respect undefiled, yet there might be no ground to suppose from thence that both or either of their persons are thereby sanctified; and the Apostle urges the cohabitation of a believer with an infidel in the state of wedlock from this ground that the unbelieving husband is sanctified by the believing wife; nevertheless here you have the influence of a believer's faith ascending from an inferior to a superior relation; from the wife to the husband who is her head, before it can descend to their offspring. And therefore we say, whatever be the nature or extent of the holiness here intended, we conceive it cannot convey to the children an immediate right to baptism; because it would then be of another nature and of a larger extent than the root and original, from whence it is derived, for it is clear by the Apostle's argument that holiness cannot be derived to the child from the sanctity of one parent only, if either father or mother be (in the sense intended by the Apostle) unholy or unclean, so will the child be also therefore for the production of an holy seed, it is necessary that both the parents be sanctified; and this the Apostle positively asserts in the first place to be done by the believing parent, although the other be an unbeliever; and then consequentially from thence argues the holiness of their children. Hence it follows, that as the children have no other holiness than what they derive from both their parents; so neither can they have any right by this holiness to any spiritual privilege but such as both their parents did also partake of; and therefore if the unbelieving parent (though sanctified by the believing parent) have not thereby a right to baptism, neither can we conceive that there is any such privilege derived to the children by their birth-holiness.

Besides if it had been the usual practice in the Apostles' days for the father or mother that did believe to bring all their children with them to be baptized; then the holiness of the believing Corinthians' children would not at all have been in question when this Epistle was written, but might have been argued from their passing under that ordinance, which represented their new birth, although they had derived no holiness from their parents by their first birth; and would have lain as an exception against the Apostle's inference, "else were your children unclean, &c." But of the sanctification of all the children of every believer by this ordinance, or any other way, than what is before mentioned, the Scripture is altogether silent.

This may also be added: that if this birth-holiness do qualify all the children of every believer for the ordinance of baptism; why not for all other ordinances, [such as] for the Lord's Supper as was practiced for a long time together? For if recourse be had to what the Scriptures speak generally of this subject, it will be found that the same qualities which do entitle any person to baptism do so also for the participation of all the ordinances and privileges of the house of God that are common to all believers.

Whosoever can and does interrogate his good conscience towards God when he is baptized (as everyone must do that makes it to himself a sign of salvation) is capable of doing the same thing in every other act of worship that he performs.

4. The arguments and inferences that are usually brought for or against infant baptism from those few instances which the Scriptures afford us of whole families being baptized are only conjectural, and therefore cannot of themselves be conclusive on either hand, yet in regard, most that treat on this subject for infant baptism do (as they conceive) improve these instances to the advantage of their argument; we think it meet (in like manner as in the cases before mentioned so in this) to show the invalidity of such inferences.

Cornelius worshipped God with all his house; the Jailor and Crispus the chief ruler of the synagogue believed God with each of their houses. The household of Stephanus addicted themselves to the ministry of the saints: so that thus far worshipping and believing runs parallel with baptism. And if Lydia had been a married person, when she believed, it is probable her husband would also have been named by the Apostle, as in like cases, inasmuch as he would have been not only a part, but the head of that baptized household.

Who can assign any probable reason why the Apostle should make mention of four or five households being baptized and no more? Or why he does so often vary in the method of his salutations, (Rom. 1:6), sometimes mentioning only particular persons of great note, other times such and the church in their house, the saints that were with them, and them belonging to Narcissus who were in the Lord; thus saluting either whole families or part of families or only particular persons in families, considered as they were in the Lord? For if it had been a usual practice to baptize all children with their parents, there were then many thousands of the Jews which believed and a great number of the Gentiles in most of the principal cities in the world; and among so many thousands, it is more than probable there would have been some thousands of households baptized; why then should the Apostle in this respect signalize one family of the Jews and three or four of the Gentiles, as particular instances in a case that was common? Whoever supposes that we do willfully debar our children from the benefit of any promise or privilege that of right belongs to the children of believing parents, they do entertain over severe thoughts of us. To be without natural affections is one of the characters of the worst of persons, in the worst of times. We do freely confess ourselves guilty before the Lord in that we have not with more circumspection and diligence trained up those that relate to us in the fear of the Lord, and do humbly and earnestly pray that our omissions herein may be remitted and that they may not redound to the prejudice of ourselves or any of ours; but with respect to that duty that is incumbent on us, we acknowledge ourselves obliged by the precepts of God to bring up our children in the nurture and admonition of the Lord, to teach them His fear both by instruction and example, and should we set light by this precept, it would demonstrate that we are more vile than the unnatural heathen that like not to retain God in their knowledge, our baptism might then be justly accompted as no baptism to us.

There are many special promises that do encourage us, as well as precepts, that do oblige us to the close pursuit of our duty herein: that God whom we serve, being jealous of His worship, threatens the visiting of the father's transgression upon the children to the third and fourth generation of them that hate Him; yet does more abundantly extend His mercy even to thousands (respecting the offspring and succeeding generations) of them that love Him and keep His commands.

When our Lord rebuked His disciples for prohibiting the access of little children that were brought to Him that He might pray over them, lay His hands upon them, and bless them, [He] does declare that "of such is the kingdom of God." And the apostle Peter, in answer to their inquiry that desired to know what they must do to be saved, does not only instruct them in the necessary duty of repentance and baptism; but does also thereto encourage them by that promise which had reference both to them and their children; if our Lord Jesus, in the forementioned place, do not respect the qualities of children (as elsewhere) as to their meekness, humility, and sincerity, and the like; but intend also that those very persons and such like appertain to the kingdom of God, and if the apostle Peter, in mentioning the aforesaid promise, do respect not only the present and succeeding generations of those Jews that heard him (in which sense the same phrase does occur in Scripture), but also the immediate offspring of his auditors; whether the promise relate to the gift of the Holy Spirit or of eternal life or any grace or privilege tending to the obtaining thereof, it is neither our concern nor our interest to confine the mercies and promises of God to a more narrow or less compass than He is pleased graciously to offer and intend them, nor to have a light esteem of them; but are obliged in duty to God and affection to our children to plead earnestly with God and use our utmost endeavors that both ourselves and our offspring may be partakers of His mercies and gracious promises; yet we cannot from either of these texts collect a sufficient warrant for us to baptize our children before they are instructed in the principles of the Christian religion.

For as to the instance in little children, it seems by the disciples forbidding them that they were brought upon some other account not so frequent as baptism must be supposed to have been, if from the beginning believers' children had been admitted thereto; and no account is given whether their parents were baptized believers or not; and as to the instance of the Apostle, if the following words and practice may be taken as an interpretation of the scope of that promise, we cannot conceive it does refer to infant baptism, because the text does presently subjoin: "Then they that gladly received his word were baptized."

That there were some believing children of believing parents in the Apostles' days is evident from the Scriptures, even such as were then in their father's family and under their parent's tuition and education; to whom the Apostle in several of his epistles to the churches gives commands to obey their parents in the Lord;

and does allure their tender years to hearken to this precept, by reminding them that it is the first command with promise. And it is recorded by him for the praise of Timothy and encouragement of parents betimes to instruct and children early to attend to godly instruction that ἀπὸ βρέφους from a child, he had known the Holy Scriptures.

The apostle John rejoiced greatly when he found of the children of the elect lady walking in the truth, and the children of her elect sister join with the Apostle in his salutation.

But that this was not generally so that all the children of believers were accounted for believers (as they would have been if they had been all baptized) may be collected from the character which the Apostle gives of persons fit to be chosen to eldership in the church which was not common to all believers; among others this is expressly one, viz. "If any...having faithful children not accused of riot or unruly;" and we may from the Apostle's writings on the same subject collect the reason of this qualification, viz. That in case the person designed for this office to teach and rule in the house of God had children capable of it; there might be first a proof of his ability, industry, and success in this work in his own family and private capacity, before he was ordained to the exercise of this authority in the church, in a public capacity, as a bishop in the house of God.

These things we have mentioned as having a direct reference unto the controversy between our brethren and us; other things that are more abstruse and prolix, which are frequently introduced into this controversy, but do not necessarily concern it, we have purposely avoided; that the distance between us and our brethren may not be by us made more wide; for it is our duty and concern so far as is possible for us (retaining a good conscience towards

God) to seek a more entire agreement and reconciliation with them.

We are not insensible that, as to the order of God's house and entire communion therein, there are some things wherein we (as well as others) are not at a full accord among ourselves as, for instance, the known principle and state of the consciences of diverse of us that have agreed in this confession is such that we cannot hold church communion with any other than baptized believers and churches constituted of such, yet some others of us have a greater liberty and freedom in our spirits that way; and therefore we have purposely omitted the mention of things of that nature, that we might concur, in giving this evidence of our agreement, both among ourselves and with other good Christians in those important articles of the Christian religion mainly insisted on by us; and this notwithstanding we all esteem it our chief concern, both among ourselves and all others, that in every place call upon the name of the Lord Jesus Christ our Lord (both theirs and ours) and love him in sincerity, to endeavor to keep the unity of the Spirit in the bond of peace; and in order thereunto, to exercise all lowliness and meekness with long-suffering, forbearing one another in love.

And we are persuaded, if the same method were introduced into frequent practice between us and our Christian friends who agree with us in all the fundamental articles of the Christian faith (though they do not so in the subject and administration of baptism), it would soon beget a better understanding and brotherly affection between us.

In the beginning of the Christian Church, when the doctrine of the baptism of Christ was not universally understood, yet those that knew only the baptism of John were the disciples of the Lord Jesus, and Apollos an eminent minister of the Gospel of Jesus.

In the beginning of the reformation of the Christian Church and recovery from that Egyptian darkness, wherein our forefathers for many generations were held in bondage, upon recourse had to the Scriptures of truth, different apprehensions were conceived, which are to this time continued, concerning the practice of this ordinance.

Let not our zeal herein be misinterpreted: that God whom we serve is jealous of His worship. By His gracious providence, the Law thereof is continued amongst us; and we are forewarned by what happened in the church of the Jews that it is necessary for every generation, and that frequently in every generation to consult the Divine oracle, compare our worship with the rule, and take heed to what doctrines we receive and practice.

If the ten commands exhibited in the Popish idolatrous service books had been received as the entire Law of God because they agree in number with His ten commands and also in the substance of nine of them, the second commandment forbidding idolatry had been utterly lost.

If Ezra and Nehemiah had not made a diligent search into the particular parts of God's Law and His worship, the feast of tabernacles (which for many centuries of years had not been duly observed, according to the institution, though it was retained in the general notion) would not have been kept in due order.

So may it be now as to many things relating to the service of God, which do retain the names proper to them in their first institution, but yet through inadvertency (where there is no sinister design) may vary in their circumstances from their first institution. And if by means of any ancient defection or of that general corruption of the service of God and interruption of His true worship and persecution of His servants by the antichristian Bishop of Rome for many generations, those who do consult the Word of God cannot yet arrive at a full and mutual satisfaction among themselves, what was the practice of the primitive Christian Church, in some points relating to the worship of God; yet inasmuch as these things are not of the essence of Christianity, but that we agree in the fundamental doctrines thereof, we do apprehend there is sufficient ground to lay aside all bitterness and prejudice, and in the spirit of love and meekness to embrace and own each other therein; leaving each other at liberty to perform such other services (wherein we cannot concur) apart unto God, according to the best of our understanding.

FINIS

Subscribers to the Confession of Faith

We the ministers and messengers of and concerned for upwards of one hundred baptized churches in England and Wales (denying Arminianism), being met together in London from the third of the seventh month to the eleventh of the same, 1689, to consider of some things that might be for the glory of God and the good of these congregations, have thought meet (for the satisfaction of all other Christians that differ from us in the point of baptism) to recommend to their perusal the confession of our faith, which confession we own, as containing the doctrine of our faith and practice, and do desire that the members of our churches respectively do furnish themselves therewith.

Hanserd Knollys	Pastor	Broken Wharf	London
William Kiffin	Pastor	Devonshire-square	London
John Harris	Pastor	Joiner's Hall	London
William Collins	Pastor	Petty France	London
Hurcules Collins	Pastor	Wapping	London
Robert Steed	Pastor	Broken Wharf	London
Leonard Harrison	Pastor	Limehouse	London
George Barret	Pastor	Mile End Green	London
Isaac Lamb	Pastor	Pennington-street	London
Richard Adams	Minister	Shad Thames	Southwark
Benjamin Keach	Pastor	Horse-lie-down	Southwark
Andrew Gifford	Pastor	Bristol, Fryars	Som. & Glouc.

Thomas Vaux	Pastor	Broadmead	Som. & Glouc.
Thomas Winnel	Pastor	Taunton	Som. & Glouc.
James Hitt	Preacher	Dalwood	Dorset
Richard Tidmarsh	Minister	Oxford City	Oxon
William Facey	Pastor	Reading	Berks
Samuel Buttall	Minister	Plymouth	Devon
Christopher Price	Minister	Abergavenny	Monmouth
Daniel Finch	Minister	Kingsworth	Herts
John Ball	Minister	Tiverton	Devon
Edmond White	Pastor	Evershall	Bedford
William Prichard	Pastor	Blaenau	Monmouth
Paul Fruin	Minister	Warwick	Warwick
Richard Ring	Pastor	Southampton	Hants
John Tomkins	Minister	Abingdon	Berks
Toby Willes	Pastor	Bridgewater	Somerset
John Carter	Pastor	Steventon	Bedford
James Webb	Pastor	Devizes	Wilts
Richard Sutton	Pastor	Tring	Herts
Robert Knight	Pastor	Stukeley	Bucks
Edward Price	Pastor	Hereford City	Hereford
William Phipps	Pastor	Exon	Devon
William Hawkins	Pastor	Dimmock	Gloucester
Samuel Ewer	Pastor	Hemstead	Herts
Edward Man	Pastor	Houndsditch	London
Charles Archer	Pastor	Hock-Norton	Oxon

In the name of and on behalf of the whole assembly.

THE BAPTIST
CATECHISM

The following page is a reproduction (with minor variations) of the
original title page of the 1809 version of the catechism
used for this book.

THE

BAPTIST CATECHISM,

OR A

BRIEF INSTRUCTION

IN THE

PRINCIPLES

OF THE

CHRISTIAN RELIGION,

AGREEABLY TO THE

CONFESSION OF FAITH

Put forth by upwards of an Hundred Congregations in Great-Britain, July 3d, 1689; and adopted by the General Association of Philadelphia September 22d, 1742, and now received by Churches of the same Denomination in the United States.

TO WHICH ARE ADDED

PROOFS OF SCRIPTURE.

WILMINGTON:

Printed & Sold by *P. Brynberg* – 1809.

~~~~~~

TO THE READER.

HAVING a desire to show our near agreement with many other Christians of whom we have great esteem; we some years since put forth a confession of our faith, almost in all points the same with that of the Assembly and Savoy which was subscribed by the Elders and Messengers of many Churches, baptized on profession of their faith; And do now put forth a short account of Christian Principles, for the instruction of our families, in most things agreeing with the Shorter Catechism of the Assembly. And this we were the rather induced to, because we have commonly made use of that catechism in our families, and the difference being not much, it will be more easily committed to memory.

~~~~~~

Q. 1. Who is the first and chiefest being?
A. God is the first[1] and chiefest being.[2]

  1. Isa. 44:6
  2. Ps. 97:9

Q. 2. Ought every one to believe there is a God?
A. Every one ought to believe there is a God,[3] and it is their great sin and folly who do not.[4]

  3. Heb. 11:6
  4. Ps. 14:1

Q. 3. How may we know there is a God?
A. The light of nature in man and the works of God plainly declare there is a God,[5] but His Word and Spirit only do it fully and effectually for the salvation of sinners.[6]

  5. Ps. 19:1-2; Rom. 1:19-20
  6. 1 Cor. 2:10; 2 Tim. 3:15

Q. 4. What is the Word of God?
A. The Holy Scriptures of the Old and New Testament are the Word of God[7] and the only certain rule of faith and obedience.[8]

  7. John 10:34-35; 2 Tim. 3:16
  8. Isa. 8:20; Eph. 2:20

Q. 5. May all men make use of the Holy Scriptures?
A. All men are not only permitted[9] but commanded and exhorted to read,[10] hear, and understand the Holy Scriptures.[11]

9. Luke 16:29
10. John 5:39
11. Matt. 15:10; Acts 8:30

Q. 6. What things are chiefly contained in the Holy Scriptures?
A. The Holy Scriptures chiefly contain what man ought to believe concerning God[12] and what duty God requires of man.[13]

12. Acts 24:14; 2 Tim. 1:13
13. Eccl. 12:13; Mic. 6:8

Q. 7. What is God?
A. God is a spirit,[14] infinite,[15] eternal,[16] and unchangeable,[17] in His being,[18] wisdom,[19] power,[20] holiness,[21] justice,[22] goodness, and truth.[23]

14. John 4:24
15. Job 11:7
16. Ps. 90:2
17. Jas. 1:17
18. Exo. 3:14
19. 1 Tim. 1:17
20. Ps. 167:5
21. Rev. 4:8
22. Ps. 84:14
23. Exo. 34:6-7

Q. 8. Are there more gods than one?
A. There is but one only, the living and true God.[24]

24. Deut. 6:4; Jer. 10:10

Q. 9. How many persons are there in the Godhead?
A. There are three persons in the Godhead, the Father, the Son, and Holy Spirit, and these three are one God, the same in essence, equal in power and glory.[25]

25. Matt. 28:19; 1 John 5:7

Q. 10. What are the decrees of God?
A. The decrees of God are His eternal purpose, according to the counsel of His will, whereby, for His own glory, He has foreordained whatsoever comes to pass.[26]

26. Rom. 9:22-23; Eph. 1:4, 11

Q. 11. How does God execute His decrees?
A. God executes His decrees in the works of creation and providence.[27]

27. Dan. 4:35; Rev. 4:11

Q. 12. What is the work of creation?
A. The work of creation is God's making all things of

nothing, by the word of His power, in the space of six days, and all very good.[28]

28. Gen. 1:1, 31; Heb. 11:3

Q. 13. *How did God create man?*
A. God created man, male and female, after His own image, in knowledge, righteousness, and holiness, with dominion over the creatures.[29]

29. Gen. 1:27-28; Eph. 4:24; Col. 3:10

Q. 14. *What are God's works of providence?*
A. God's works of providence are His most holy,[30] wise,[31] and powerful preserving[32] and governing all His creatures and all their actions.[33]

30. Ps. 145:17
31. Isa. 28:29
32. Heb. 1:3
33. Ps. 103:19; Matt. 10:29

Q. 15. *What special act of providence did God exercise towards man in the estate wherein he was created?*
A. When God had created man, He entered into a covenant of life with him upon condition of perfect obedience, forbidding him to eat of the tree of knowledge of good and evil upon pain of death.[34]

34. Gen. 2:17; Gal. 3:12

Q. 16. Did our first parents continue in that estate wherein they were created?
A. Our first parents being left to the freedom of their own will fell from the estate wherein they were created by sinning against God.[35]

35. Eccl. 7:29; Rom. 3:23

Q. 17. What is sin?
A. Sin is any want of conformity unto or transgression of the Law of God.[36]

36. 1 John 3:4

Q. 18. What was the sin whereby our first parents fell from the estate wherein they were created?
A. The sin whereby our first parents fell from the estate wherein they were created was their eating the forbidden fruit.[37]

37. Gen. 3:6, 12-13

Q. 19. Did all mankind fall in Adam's first transgression?
A. The covenant being made with Adam, not only for himself but for his posterity, all mankind descending from him by ordinary generation sinned in him and fell with him in his first transgression.[38]

38. Gen. 2:16-17; Rom. 5:12; 1 Cor. 15:21-22

Q. 20. Into what estate did the Fall bring mankind?
A. The Fall brought mankind into a estate of sin and misery.[39]

39. Ps. 51:5; Rom. 5:17-18

Q. 21. Wherein consists the sinfulness of that estate whereinto man fell?
A. The sinfulness of that estate whereinto man fell consists in the guilt of Adam's first sin,[40] the want of original righteousness,[41] and the corruption of his whole nature, which is commonly called original sin,[42] together with all actual transgressions which proceed from it.[43]

40. Rom. 5:19
41. Rom. 3:10
42. Job 14:4
43. Isa. 64:6; Matt. 15:19; Jas. 1:14

Q. 22. What is the misery of that estate whereinto man fell?
A. All mankind by their fall lost communion with God,[44] are under His wrath[45] and curse,[46] and so made liable to all the miseries in this life,[47] to death itself,[48] and to the pains of hell forever.[49]

44. Gen. 3:8, 24
45. Eph. 2:3
46. Gal. 3:10
47. Job 14:1

48. Rom. 6:23
49. Ps. 9:17; Matt. 25:46

Q. 23. Did God leave all mankind to perish in the estate of sin and misery?
A. God, having out of His mere good pleasure, from all eternity, elected some to everlasting life,[50] did enter into a Covenant of Grace to deliver them out of the estate of sin and misery and to bring them into a estate of salvation by a redeemer.[51]

50. 2 Thess. 2:13
51. Isa. 49:8; Rom. 5:21

Q. 24. Who is the Redeemer of God's elect?
A. The only Redeemer of God's elect is the Lord Jesus Christ,[52] who, being the eternal Son of God,[53] became man,[54] and so was and continues to be God and man, in two distinct natures,[55] and one person forever.[56]

52. Gal. 3:13; 1 Tim. 2:5
53. 2 John 3
54. John 1:14
55. Rom. 9:5; 1 Tim. 3:16
56. Col. 2:9; Heb. 7:24

Q. 25. How did Christ, being the Son of God, become man?
A. Christ, the Son of God, became man by taking to Himself a true body[57] and a reasonable soul,[58]

being conceived by the power of the Holy Spirit in the womb of the Virgin Mary and born of her[59] yet without sin.[60]

57. Heb. 2:14; 10:5
58. John 12:27
59. Luke 1:31, 35
60. Heb. 4:15; 7:20

Q. 26. *What offices does Christ execute as our Redeemer?*
A. Christ as our Redeemer executes the offices of a prophet,[61] of a priest,[62] and of a king,[63] both in His estate of humiliation and exaltation.

61. Acts 3:22
62. Heb 5:6
63. Ps. 2:6

Q. 27. *How does Christ execute the office of a prophet?*
A. Christ executes the office of a prophet in revealing to us,[64] by His Word[65] and Spirit,[66] the will of God for our salvation.

64. John 1:18
65. John 15:15
66. John 14:26

Q. 28. *How does Christ execute the office of a priest?*
A. Christ executes the office of a priest in His once offering up of Himself a sacrifice to satisfy Divine

justice[67] and reconcile us to God[68] and in making
continual intercession for us.[69]

67. Eph. 5:2; Heb. 9:28
68. Heb. 2:17
69. Heb. 7:25

Q. 29. How does Christ execute the office of a king?
A. Christ executes the office of a king in subduing
us to Himself,[70] in ruling[71] and defending us,[72] and
in restraining[73] and conquering all His and our
enemies.[74]

70. Ps. 110:3
71. Matt. 2:6
72. Zech. 9:15
73. Ps. 76:10
74. 1 Cor. 15:25

Q. 30. Wherein did Christ's humiliation consist?
A. Christ's humiliation consisted in His being born
and that in a low condition,[75] made under the Law,[76]
undergoing the miseries of this life,[77] the wrath of
God[78] and the cursed death of the cross,[79] in being
buried,[80] and continuing under the power of death
for a time.[81]

75. Luke 2:7
76. Gal. 4:4
77. Isa. 53:3
78. Matt. 27:46; Luke 22:44
79. Phil. 2:8

80. 1 Cor. 15:4
81. Matt. 12:40

Q. 31. Wherein consists Christ's exaltation?
A. Christ's exaltation consists in His rising again
from the dead on the third day,[82] in ascending up
into heaven,[83] in sitting at the right hand of God the
Father,[84] and in coming to judge the world at the last
day.[85]

82. 1 Cor. 15:4
83. Acts 1:11
84. Mark 16:19; Eph. 1:20
85. Acts 17:31

*Q. 32. How are we made partakers of the redemption
purchased by Christ?*
A. We are made partakers of the redemption
purchased by Christ by the effectual application of it
to us[86] by His Holy Spirit.[87]

86. Gal. 4:5
87. Titus 3:5-6

*Q. 33. How does the Spirit apply to us the redemption
purchased by Christ?*
A. The Spirit applies to us the redemption
purchased by Christ by working faith in us[88] and
thereby uniting us to Christ[89] in our effectual
calling.[90]

88. Eph. 2:8
89. Eph. 3:17
90. 1 Cor. 1:9

Q. 34. What is effectual calling?

A. Effectual calling is the work of God's Spirit,[91] whereby convincing us of our sin and misery,[92] enlightening our minds in the knowledge of Christ,[93] and renewing our wills,[94] He does persuade and enable us to embrace Jesus Christ freely offered to us in the Gospel.[95]

91. 2 Tim. 1:9
92. Acts 2:37
93. Acts 2:18
94. Ezek. 36:26-27
95. John 6:44-45

Q. 35. What benefits do they that are effectually called partake of in this life?

A. They that are effectually called do in this life partake of justification,[96] adoption,[97] sanctification,[98] and the several benefits which in this life do either accompany or flow from them.[99]

96. Rom. 8:30
97. Gal. 3:26
98. 1 Cor. 6:11
99. 1 Cor. 1:30

Q. 36. What is justification?

A. Justification is an act of God's free grace,[100]

wherein He pardons all our sins[101] and accepts us as righteous in His sight,[102] only for the righteousness of Christ imputed to us[103] and received by faith alone.[104]

100. Rom. 3:24
101. Eph. 1:7
102. 2 Cor. 5:21
103. Rom. 4:6
104. Rom. 3:22

Q. 37. What is adoption?
A. Adoption is an act of God's free grace,[105] whereby we are received into the number and have a right to all the privileges of the sons of God.[106]

105. 1 John 3:1
106. John 1:12; Rom. 8:17

Q. 38. What is sanctification?
A. Sanctification is the work of God's free grace,[107] whereby we are renewed in the whole man after the image of God[108] and are enabled more and more to die unto sin and live unto righteousness.[109]

107. 2 Thess. 2:13
108. Eph. 4:23-24
109. Rom. 6:11

Q. 39. What are the benefits which in this life do accompany or flow from justification, adoption, and sanctification?
A. The benefits which in this life do accompany or flow from justification, adoption, and sanctification are assurance of God's love, peace of conscience,[110] joy in the Holy Spirit,[111] increase of grace,[112] and perseverance therein to the end.[113]

110. Rom. 5:1-2, 5
111. Rom. 14:7
112. Pro. 4:18
113. 1 Pet. 1:5

Q. 40. What benefits do believers receive from Christ at their death?
A. The souls of believers are at their death made perfect in holiness[114] and do immediately pass into glory,[115] and their bodies, being still united to Christ,[116] do rest in their graves[117] till the resurrection.[118]

114. Heb. 12:23
115. 2 Cor. 5:8; Phil. 1:23
116. 1 Thess. 4:14
117. Isa. 57:2
118. Job 19:26

Q. 41. What benefits do believers receive from Christ at the resurrection?
A. At the resurrection, believers being raised up in

glory[119] shall be openly acknowledged and acquitted in the day of judgment[120] and made perfectly blessed both in soul and body in the full enjoyment of God[121] to all eternity.[122]

119. 1 Cor. 15:43
120. Matt. 10:32; Acts 3:19
121. 1 John 3:2
122. 1 Thess. 4:17

Q. 42. But what shall be done to the wicked at their death?
A. The souls of the wicked shall at their death be cast into the torments of hell,[123] and their bodies lie in their graves till the resurrection and judgment of the great day.[124]

123. Luke 16:22-24
124. Ps. 49:14

Q. 43. What shall be done to the wicked at the day of judgment?
A. At the day of judgment, the bodies of the wicked being raised out of their graves shall be sentenced together with their souls to unspeakable torments, with the devil and his angels forever.[125]

125. Dan. 12:2; Matt. 25:41; John 5:28-29; 2 Thess. 1:9

Q. 44. *What is the duty which God requires of man?*
A. The duty which God requires of man is obedience to His revealed will.[126]

126. Ps. 119:4; Mic. 6:8

Q. 45. *What did God at first reveal to man for the rule of his obedience?*
A. The rule which God at first revealed to man for his obedience was the moral law.[127]

127. Rom. 2:14-15

Q. 46. *Where is the moral law summarily comprehended?*
A. The moral law is summarily comprehended in the Ten Commandments.[128]

128. Deut. 10:4; Matt. 19:17

Q. 47. *What is the sum of the Ten Commandments?*
A. The sum of the Ten Commandments is to love the Lord our God with all our heart, with all our soul, with all our strength, and with all our mind; and our neighbor as ourselves.[129]

104. Matt. 22:37-40

Q. 48. What is the preface to the Ten Commandments?
A. The preface to the Ten Commandments is in these words, *I am the Lord thy God, which have brought thee out of the land of Egypt, out of the house of bondage.*[130]

130. Exo. 20:2

Q. 49. What does the preface to the Ten Commandments teach us?
A. The preface to the Ten Commandments teaches us that because God is the Lord and our God and Redeemer, therefore we are bound to keep all His commandments.[131]

131. Deut. 11:1; Luke 1:74-75

Q. 50. Which is the first commandment?
A. The first commandment is, "Thou shalt have no other gods before me."[132]

132. Exo. 20:3

Q. 51. What is required in the first commandment?
A. The first commandment requires us to know and acknowledge God to be the only true God and our God,[133] and to worship and glorify Him accordingly.[134]

133. Deut. 26:17; 1 Chr. 28:9
134. Ps. 29:2; Matt. 4:10

Q. 52. What is forbidden in the first commandment?
A. The first commandment forbids the denying[135] or not worshipping the true God as God[136] and our God,[137] and the giving that worship and glory to any other, which is due unto Him alone.[138]

135. Josh. 24:27
136. Rom. 1:20-21
137. Isa. 59:13
138. Rom. 1:25

Q. 53. What are we especially taught by these words, "before me" in the first commandment?
A. These words "before me" in the first commandment teach us that God who sees all things takes notice of and is much displeased with the sin of having any other god.[139]

139. Ps. 44:20-21

Q. 54. Which is the second commandment?
A. The second commandment is, "Thou shalt not make unto thee any graven image, or any likeness of any thing that is in heaven above, or that is in the earth beneath, or that is in the water under the earth. Thou shalt not bow down thyself to them, nor serve them: for I the LORD thy God am a jealous God, visiting the iniquity of the fathers upon the children unto the third and fourth generation of them that hate me;

And shewing mercy unto thousands of them that love me, and keep my commandments."[140]

140. Exo. 20:4-6

Q. 55. What is required in the second commandment?
A. The second commandment requires the receiving, observing, and keeping pure and entire, all such religious worship and ordinances, as God has appointed in His Word.[141]

141. Deut. 12:32; 32:46; Matt. 28:20

Q. 56. What is forbidden in the second commandment?
A. The second commandment forbids the worshipping of God by images[142] or any other way not appointed in His Word.[143]

142. Deut. 4:15-16
143. Col. 2:21-22

Q. 57. What are the reasons annexed to the second commandment?
A. The reasons annexed to the second commandment are God's sovereignty over us,[144] His propriety in us,[145] and the zeal He has to His own worship.[146]

144. Ps. 95:2-3
145. Ps. 14:11
146. Exo. 34:14

Q. 58. Which is the third commandment?
A. The third commandment is, "Thou shalt not take the name of the LORD thy God in vain; for the LORD will not hold him guiltless that taketh his name in vain."[147]

147. Exo. 20:7

Q. 59. What is required in the third commandment?
A. The third commandment requires the holy and reverent use of God's name,[148] titles,[149] attributes,[150] ordinances,[151] word,[152] and works.[153]

148. Ps. 111:9; Matt. 6:9
149. Deut 28:58; Ps. 68:4
150. Deut. 32:3-4
151. Eccl. 5:1
152. Ps. 138: 2
153. Job 36:24

Q. 60. What is forbidden in the third commandment?
A. The third commandment forbids all profaning and abusing of anything whereby God makes Himself known.[154]

154. Mal. 1:6-7

Q. 61. What is the reason annexed to the third commandment?
A. The reason annexed to the third commandment is that however the breakers of this commandment

may escape punishment from men, yet the Lord our God will not suffer them to escape His righteous judgment.[155]

155. Deut. 58:59; Mal. 2:2

Q. 62. Which is the fourth commandment?
A. The fourth commandment is, "Remember the sabbath day, to keep it holy. Six days shalt thou labour, and do all thy work: But the seventh day is the sabbath of the LORD thy God: in it thou shalt not do any work, thou, nor thy son, nor thy daughter, thy manservant, nor thy maidservant, nor thy cattle, nor thy stranger that is within thy gates: For in six days the LORD made heaven and earth, the sea, and all that in them is, and rested the seventh day: wherefore the LORD blessed the sabbath day, and hallowed it."[156]

156. Exo. 20:8-11

Q. 63. What is required in the fourth commandment?
A. The fourth commandment requires the keeping holy to God one whole day in seven to be a sabbath to Himself.[157]

157. Lev. 19:30; Deut. 5:12

Q. 64. Which day of the seven has God appointed to be the weekly Sabbath?

A. Before the resurrection of Christ, God appointed the seventh day of the week to be the weekly Sabbath,[158] and the first day of the week ever since, to continue to the end of the world, which is the Christian Sabbath.[159]

158. Exo. 31:15
159. John 20:19; Acts 20:7; 1 Cor. 16:1-2; Rev. 1:10

Q. 65. How is the Sabbath to be sanctified?

A. The Sabbath is to be sanctified by a holy resting all that day even from such worldly employments and recreations as are lawful on other days[160] and spending the whole time in the public and private exercises of God's worship,[161] except so much as is to be taken up in the works of necessity and mercy.[162]

160. Lev. 22:3; Isa. 58:13
161. Ps. 92; Isa. 66:23
162. Matt. 12:11-12

Q. 66. What is forbidden in the fourth commandment?

A. The fourth commandment forbids the omission or careless performance of the duties required[163] and the profaning the day by idleness[164] or doing that which is in itself sinful[165] or by unnecessary thoughts, words, or works about worldly employments or recreations.[166]

163. Ezek. 22:26
164. Acts 20:9
165. Ezek. 23:38
166. Neh. 13:15, 17

Q. 67. What are the reasons annexed to the fourth commandment?

A. The reasons annexed to the fourth commandment are God's allowing us six days of the week for our own lawful employments,[167] His challenging a special property in the seventh,[168] His own example,[169] and His blessing the Sabbath Day.[170]

167. Exo. 34:21
168. Exo. 35:2
169. Exo. 21:16-17
170. Gen. 2:3

Q. 68. Which is the fifth commandment?

A. The fifth commandment is, "Honour thy father and thy mother: that thy days may be long upon the land which the LORD thy God giveth thee."[171]

171. Exo. 20:12

Q. 69. What is required in the fifth commandment?

A. The fifth commandment requires the preserving the honor and performing the duties belonging to everyone in their several places and relations, as superiors,[172] inferiors,[173] or equals.[174]

172. Rom. 13:1; 1 Pet. 2:17

173. Eph. 5:21-22; Eph. 6:1, 5, 9; Col. 3:19
174. Rom. 12:10

Q. 70. What is forbidden in the fifth commandment?
A. The fifth commandment forbids the neglecting of[175] or doing anything against the honor or duty which belong to everyone in their several places and relations.[176]

175. Deut. 21:18-21; Pro. 30:17
176. Rom. 13:7-8

Q. 71. What is the reason annexed to the fifth commandment?
A. The reason annexed to the fifth commandment, is a promise of long life and prosperity (as far as it shall serve for God's glory and their own good) to all such as keep this commandment.[177]

177. Eph. 6:2-3

Q. 72. Which is the sixth commandment?
A. The sixth commandment is, "Thou shalt not kill."[178]

178. Exo. 20:13

Q. 73. What is required in the sixth commandment?
A. The sixth commandment requires all lawful endeavours to preserve our own life[179] and the life of others.[180]

179. Job 2:4; Eph. 5:28-29
180. Ps. 82:3-4; Pro. 24:11

Q. 74. What is forbidden in the sixth commandment?
A. The sixth commandment absolutely forbids
the taking away our own life[181] or the life of our
neighbor unjustly or whatsoever tends thereto.[182]

181. Acts 16:28
182. Gen. 9:6

Q. 75. Which is the seventh commandment?
A. The seventh commandment is, "Thou shalt not
commit adultery."[183]

183. Exo. 20:14

Q. 76. What is required in the seventh commandment?
A. The seventh commandment requires the
preservation of our own[184] and our neighbor's
chastity[185] in heart,[186] speech,[187] and behavior.[188]

184. 1 Cor. 7:2
185. 1 Cor. 6:18
186. Matt. 5:28; 2 Tim. 2:22
187. Col. 4:6
188. 1 Pet. 3:2

Q. 77. What is forbidden in the seventh commandment?
A. The seventh commandment forbids all unchaste
thoughts,[189] words,[190] and actions.[191]

189. Job 31:1
190. Eph. 5:4
191. Rom. 13:13; Eph. 5:3

Q. 78. Which is the eighth commandment?
A. The eighth commandment is, "Thou shalt not steal."[192]

192. Exo. 20:15

Q. 79. What is required in the eighth commandment?
A. The eighth commandment requires the lawful procuring and furthering the wealth and outward estate of ourselves[193] and others.[194]

193. Gen. 30:30; Pro. 27:23
194. Lev. 25:35; Deut. 22:1, 3-4

Q. 80. What is forbidden in the eighth commandment?
A. The eighth commandment forbids whatsoever does or may unjustly hinder our own[194] or our neighbor's wealth or outward estate.[195]

194. Pro. 28:19; 1 Tim. 5:8
195. Pro. 23:20-21; Eph. 4:28

Q. 81. Which is the ninth commandment?
A. The ninth commandment is, "Thou shalt not bear false witness against thy neighbor."[196]

196. Exo. 20:16

Q. 82. What is required in the ninth commandment?
A. The ninth commandment requires the maintaining and promoting of truth between man and man,[197] and of our own[198] and our neighbor's good name,[199] especially in witness bearing.[200]

197. Zech. 8:16
198. Eccl. 7:21
199. 3 John 12
200. Pro. 14:25

Q. 83. What is forbidden in the ninth commandment?
A. The ninth commandment forbids whatsoever is prejudicial to truth[201] or injurious to our own[202] or our neighbor's good name.[203]

201. Eph. 4:25
202. Pro. 10:7
203. Ps. 15:3

Q. 84. Which is the tenth commandment?
A. The tenth commandment is, "Thou shalt not covet thy neighbour's house, thou shalt not covet thy neighbour's wife, nor his manservant, nor his maidservant, nor his ox, nor his ass, nor any thing that is thy neighbour's."[204]

204. Exo. 20:17

Q. 85. What is required in the tenth commandment?
A. The tenth commandment requires full

contentment with our own condition[205] with a right and charitable frame of spirit towards our neighbor and all that is his.[206]

205. 1 Tim. 6:6; Heb. 13:5
206. Rom. 12:15; 1 Cor. 13:4, 7

Q. 86. What is forbidden in the tenth commandment?
A. The tenth commandment forbids all discontentment with our own estate,[207] envying or grieving at the good of our neighbor,[208] and all inordinate motions and affections to anything that is his.[209]

207. 1 Cor. 10:10
208. Matt. 20:15; Jas. 5:9
209. 1 Kgs. 21:4; Col. 3:15

Q. 87. Is any man able perfectly to keep the commandments of God?
A. No mere man since the Fall is able in this life perfectly to keep the commandments of God,[210] but does daily break them in thought,[211] word,[212] or deed.[213]

210. Eccl. 7:20; 1 John 1:8
211. Gen. 6:5
212. Jas. 3:8
213. Jas. 3:2

Q. 88. Are all transgressions of the Law equally heinous?

A. Some sins in themselves, and by reason of several aggravations are more heinous in the sight of God than others.[214]

214. Ezek. 8:13; John 19:11; 1 John 5:16

Q. 89. What does every sin deserve?

A. Every sin deserves God's wrath and curse both in this life and that which is to come.[215]

215. Ps. 11:6; Pro. 3:33; Eph. 5:6; Rev. 21:8

Q. 90. What does God require of us that we may escape His wrath and curse due to us for sin?

A. To escape the wrath and curse of God due to us for sin, God requires of us faith in Jesus Christ,[216] repentance unto life,[217] with the diligent use of all the outward means whereby Christ communicates to us the benefits of redemption.[218]

216. Acts 16:30-31
217. Acts 27:30
218. Pro. 2:3-5; 8:34-35

Q. 91. What is faith in Jesus Christ?

A. Faith in Jesus Christ is a saving grace,[219] whereby we receive[220] and rest upon Him alone for salvation, as He is offered to us in the Gospel.[221]

219. Heb. 10:39
220. John 1:12
221. Phil. 3:9

Q. 92. *What is repentance unto life?*

A. Repentance unto life is a saving grace,[222] whereby a sinner, out of a true sense of his sins[223] and apprehension of the mercy of God in Christ,[224] does, with grief and hatred of his sin, turn from it unto God,[225] with full purpose of and endeavor after new obedience.[226]

222. Acts 11:18
223. Acts 2:37
224. Joel 2:13
225. Jer 31:18-19
226. Ps. 119:59-60

Q. 93. *What are the outward means whereby Christ communicates to us the benefits of redemption?*

A. The outward and ordinary means whereby Christ communicates to us the benefits of redemption are His ordinances, especially the Word, baptism, the Lord's Supper, and prayer; all which means are made effectual to the elect for salvation.[227]

227. Ps. 92:13-14; Acts 2:41-42

Q. 94. *How is the Word made effectual to salvation?*

A. The Spirit of God makes the reading,[228] but especially the preaching of the Word, an effectual means of convincing and converting sinners[229] and

of building them up in holiness and comfort,[230]
through faith unto salvation.[231]

228. Neh. 8:8; Ps. 19:7
229. Ps. 51:13; Rom. 10:14, 17
230. Acts 20:32; 1 Cor. 14:3
231. Rom. 1:16

Q. 95. How is the Word to be read and heard that it may become effectual to salvation?
A. That the Word may become effectual to salvation, we must attend thereunto with diligence,[232] preparation,[233] and prayer;[234] receive it with faith[235] and love;[236] lay it up in our hearts;[237] and practice it in our lives.[238]

232. 1 Tim. 4:13
233. 1 Pet. 2:1-2
234. Ps. 119:18
235. Heb. 4:2
236. 2 Thess. 2:10
237. Ps. 119:11
238. Jas. 1:25

Q. 96. How do baptism and the Lord's Supper become effectual means of salvation?
A. Baptism and the Lord's Supper become effectual means of salvation, not from any virtue in them or him that does adminster them,[239] but only by the blessing of Christ[240] and the working of His Spirit in those who by faith receive them.[241]

239. 1 Cor. 3:7; 1 Pet. 3:21
240. 1 Cor. 3:6
241. 1 Cor. 12:13

Q. 97. What is baptism?

A. Baptism is an ordinance of the New Testament, instituted by Jesus Christ[242] to be unto the party baptized a sign of his fellowship with Him in His death and burial and resurrection,[243] of his being engrafted into Him,[244] of remission of sins,[245] and of his giving up himself unto God through Jesus Christ to live and walk in newness of life.[246]

242. Matt. 28:19
243. Rom. 6:3 ; Col. 2:12
244. Gal. 3:27
245. Mark 1:4; Acts 22:16
246. Rom. 6:4-5

Q. 98. To whom is baptism to be administered?

A. Baptism is to be administered to all those who actually profess repentance toward God,[247] faith in, and obedience to our Lord Jesus Christ; and to none other.[248]

247. Matt. 3:6; Acts 2:38
248. Mark 16:16; Acts 8:12, 36-37; 10:47-48

Q. 99. Are the infants of such as are professing believers to be baptized?

A. The infants of such as are professing believers are not to be baptized because there is neither command nor example in the Holy Scriptures or certain consequence from them to baptize such.[249]

249. Exo. 23:13; Pro. 30:6; Luke 3:7-8

Q. 100. How is baptism rightly administered?
A. Baptism is rightly administered by immersion or dipping the whole body of the party in water[250] in the name of the Father and of the Son and of the Holy Spirit, according to Christ's institution[251] and the practice of the apostles,[252] and not by sprinkling or pouring of water or dipping some parts of the body, after the tradition of men.[253]

250. Matt. 3:16; John 3:23;
251. Matt. 28:19-20
252. John 4:1-2
253. Acts 8:38-39

Q. 101. What is the duty of such who are rightly baptized?
A. It is the duty of those who are rightly baptized to give up themselves to some particular and orderly church of Jesus Christ[254] that they may walk in all the commandments and ordinances of the Lord blameless.[255]

254. Acts 2:47; 9:26
255. Luke 1:6; 1 Pet. 2:5

Q. 102. What is the Lord's Supper?
A. The Lord's Supper is an ordinance of the New
Testament instituted by Jesus Christ, wherein by
giving and receiving bread and wine, according
to His appointment, His death is showed forth,[256]
and the worthy receivers are, not after a corporal
and carnal manner, but by faith made partakers of
His body and blood, with all His benefits, to their
spiritual nourishment and growth in grace.[257]

256. 1 Cor. 11:23-26
257. 1 Cor. 10:16

Q. 103. Who are the proper subjects of this ordinance?
A. They who have been baptized upon a personal
profession of their faith in Jesus Christ and
repentance from dead works.[258]

258. Acts 2:41-42

*Q. 104. What is required to the worthy receiving of the
Lord's Supper?*
A. It is required of them that would worthily
partake of the Lord's Supper that they examine
themselves of their knowledge to discern the Lord's
body,[259] of their faith to feed upon Him,[260] of their
repentance,[261] love,[262] and new obedience;[263] lest
coming unworthily, they eat and drink judgment to
themselves.[264]

259. 1 Cor. 11:28
260. 2 Cor. 13:5
261. 1 Cor. 11:31
262. 1 Cor. 11:18, 20
263. 1 Cor. 5:8
264. 1 Cor. 11:29

Q. 105. What is prayer?

A. Prayer is an offering up our desires to God,[265] by the assistance of the Holy Spirit,[266] for things agreeable to His will,[267] in the name of Christ,[268] believing,[269] with confession of our sins,[270] and thankful acknowledgment of His mercies.[271]

265. Ps. 62:8
266. Rom. 8:26
267. Rom. 8:27
268. John 16:23
269. Matt. 21:22
270. Dan. 9:4
271. Phil. 4:6

Q. 106. What rule has God given for our direction in prayer?

A. The whole Word of God is of use to direct us in prayer,[272] but the special rule of direction is that prayer, which Christ taught His disciples, commonly called *The Lord's Prayer*.[273]

272. Luke 11:1; 2 Tim. 3:16-17; 1 John 5:4
273. Matt. 6:9

Q. 107. What does the preface to the Lord's Prayer teach us?

A. The preface of the Lord's Prayer, which is, "Our Father, which art in heaven,"[274] teaches us to draw near to God with all holy reverence and confidence as children to a father, able and ready to help us,[275] and that we should pray with and for others.[220]

274. Matt. 6:9
275. Isa. 64:8; Matt. 7:11; Rom. 8:15
276. Acts 12:5; 1 Tim. 2:1-2

Q. 108. What do we pray for in the first petition?

A. In the first petition, which is, "Hallowed be thy name,"[277] we pray that God would enable us and others to glorify Him in all that whereby He makes Himself known,[278] and that He would dispose all things to His own glory.[279]

277. Matt. 6:9
278. Ps. 67:1-2
279. Ps. 83:18; Rom. 11:36

Q. 109. What do we pray for in the second petition?

A. In the second petition, which is, "Thy kingdom come,"[280] we pray that Satan's kingdom may be destroyed,[281] and that the kingdom of grace may be advanced,[282] ourselves and others brought into it and kept in it,[283] and that the kingdom of glory may be hastened.[284]

280. Matt. 6:10
281. Ps. 68:1, 18
282. Ps. 2:18; Rom. 10:2
283. John 17:20-21; 2 Thess. 3:1
284. Rev. 22:20

Q. 110. What do we pray for in the third petition?
A. In the third petition, which is, "Thy will be done in earth, as it is in heaven,"[285] we pray that God, by His grace, would make us able and willing to know, obey,[286] and submit to His will in all things,[287] as the angels do in heaven.[288]

285. Matt. 6:10
286. Ps. 119:34, 36
287. Luke 22:42; Acts 21:14
288. Ps. 103:20-21

Q. 111. What do we pray for in the fourth petition?
A. In the fourth petition, which is, "Give us this day our daily bread,"[289] we pray that, of God's free gift, we may receive a competent portion of the good things of this life[290] and enjoy His blessing with them.[291]

289. Matt. 6:11
290. Pro. 30:8
291. Exo. 23:25; 1 Tim. 4:4-5

Q. 112. What do we pray for in the fifth petition?
A. In the fifth petition, which is, "And forgive us our debts, as we forgive our debtors,"[292] we pray that

God for Christ's sake would freely pardon all our sins,[293] which we are the rather encouraged to ask, because by His grace we are enabled from the heart to forgive others.[294]

292. Matt. 6:12
293. Ps. 51:1-2, 7
294 Matt. 6:14; Luke 11:4

Q. 113. What do we pray for in the sixth petition?
A. In the sixth petition, which is, "And lead us not into temptation, but deliver us from evil,"[295] we pray that God would either keep us from being tempted to sin[296] or support and deliver us when we are tempted.[297]

295. Matt. 6:13
296. Matt. 26:41
297. 1 Cor. 10:13; 2 Cor. 12:7-8

Q. 114. What does the conclusion of the Lord's Prayer teach us?
A. The conclusion of the Lord's Prayer, which is, "For thine is the kingdom, and the power, and the glory, for ever. Amen,"[298] teaches us to take our encouragement in prayer from God only[299] and in our prayers to praise Him, ascribing kingdom,

power, and glory to Him;[300] and in testimony of our desire and assurance to be heard we say, *Amen.*[301]

298. Matt. 6:13
299 Dan. 9:4, 9, 18-19
300. 1 Chr. 29:11, 23
301. 1 Cor. 14:16; Rev. 22:20

THE LORD'S PRAYER

OUR Father which art in heaven, Hallowed be thy name. Thy kingdom come, Thy will be done in earth, as it is in heaven. Give us this day our daily bread. And forgive us our debts, as we forgive our debtors. And lead us not into temptation, but deliver us from evil: For thine is the kingdom, and the power, and the glory, for ever. AMEN.

THE APOSTLE'S CREED

I BELIEVE in God the Father Almighty, Maker of heaven and earth; and in Jesus Christ His only Son, our Lord, who was conceived by the Holy Ghost, born of the Virgin Mary, suffered under Pontius Pilate, was crucified, dead, and buried; He descended into hell;* the third day, He arose again from the dead; He ascended into heaven, and sits on the right hand of God the Father Almighty, from whence He shall come to judge the quick and the dead. I believe in the Holy Ghost, the holy catholic[†] Church, the communion of saints, the forgiveness of sins, the resurrection of the body, and the life everlasting. AMEN.

* Continued in the state of the dead, and under the power of death, till the third day.
[†] Universal

THE LAW OF GOD,

CONTAINED IN

THE TEN COMMANDMENTS

GIVEN BY GOD AT MOUNT SINAI,

Exodus, Chapters 19 and 20

And it came to pass on the third day in the morning, that there were thunders and lightnings, and a thick cloud upon the mount, and the voice of the trumpet exceeding loud; so that all the people that was in the camp trembled. And Moses brought forth the people out of the camp to meet with God; and they stood at the nether part of the mount. And mount Sinai was altogether on a smoke, because the LORD descended upon it in fire: and the smoke thereof ascended as the smoke of a furnace, and the whole mount quaked greatly. And when the voice of the trumpet sounded long, and waxed louder and louder, Moses spake, and God answered him by a voice …

And God spake all these words, saying, I am the LORD thy God, which have brought thee out of the land of Egypt, out of the house of bondage.

I. Thou shalt have no other gods before me.

II. Thou shalt not make unto thee any graven image, or any likeness of any thing that is in heaven above, or that is in the earth beneath, or that is in the water under the earth. Thou shalt not bow down thyself to them, nor serve them: for I the LORD thy God am a jealous God, visiting the iniquity of the fathers upon the children unto the third and fourth generation of them that hate me; And shewing mercy unto thousands of them that love me, and keep my commandments.

III. Thou shalt not take the name of the LORD thy God in vain; for the LORD will not hold him guiltless that taketh his name in vain.

IV. Remember the sabbath day, to keep it holy. Six days shalt thou labour, and do all thy work: But the seventh day is the sabbath of the LORD thy God: in it thou shalt not do any work, thou, nor thy son, nor thy daughter, thy manservant, nor thy maidservant, nor thy cattle, nor thy stranger that is within thy gates: For in six days the LORD made heaven and earth, the sea, and all that in them is, and rested the seventh day: wherefore the LORD blessed the sabbath day, and hallowed it.

V. Honour thy father and thy mother: that thy days may be long upon the land which the LORD thy God giveth thee.

VI. Thou shalt not kill.

VII. Thou shalt not commit adultery.

VIII. Thou shalt not steal.

IX. Thou shalt not bear false witness against thy neighbour.

X. Thou shalt not covet thy neighbour's house, thou shalt not covet thy neighbour's wife, nor his manservant, nor his maidservant, nor his ox, nor his ass, nor any thing that is thy neighbour's.

THE SPIRIT OF THE WHOLE LAW

MASTER, which is the great commandment in the law?

Jesus said unto him, Thou shalt love the Lord thy God with all thy heart, and with all thy soul, and with all thy mind. This is the first and great commandment.

And the second is like unto it, Thou shalt love thy neighbour as thyself. On these two commandments hang all the law and the prophets.

MATTHEW 22:36-40

OUR SAVIOUR'S COMMANDMENT

A NEW commandment I give unto you, That ye love one another; as I have loved you, that ye also love one another.

By this shall all men know that ye are my disciples, if ye have love one to another.

JOHN 13:34-35

FINIS

—— End Notes ——

(NOTE: There are minor edits to a few quotes.)

a. **Smiths.** "The BCF Assistant." *The BCF Assistant*. 25 June 2009. 02 Feb. 2012. <http://www.vor.org/rbdisk/bcfassis.htm>.

b. **Ryle, J. C.** *Holiness: Its Nature, Hindrances, Difficulties, and Roots*. Moscow: Charles Nolan, 2001. xvi.

c. *The Baptist Confession of Faith 1689, Or, The Second London Confession with Scripture Proofs*. Ed. Peter Masters. London: Wakeman Trust, 1998. 3.

d. **Watson, Thomas, and Samuel Lee.** *The Bible and the Closet*. Ed. John Overton Choules. Boston: Gould, Kendall & Lincoln, 1842. 42-43.

e. **Spurgeon, Charles**. "The Immutability of God." *The Spurgeon Archive*. The Spurgeon Archive, 2001. 26 Jan. 2012. <http://www.spurgeon.org/sermons/0001.htm>.

f. **Spurgeon, Charles**. "Divine Sovereignty." *The Spurgeon Archive*. The Spurgeon Archive, 2001. 26 Jan. 2012. <http://www.spurgeon.org/sermons/0077.htm>.

g. **Watson, Thomas**. *A Body of Divinity: Contained in Sermons upon the Westminster Assembly's Catechism*. Edinburgh: Banner of Truth Trust, 2000. 118.

h. **Watson, Thomas**. *A Body of Divinity: Contained in Sermons upon the Westminster Assembly's Catechism.* Edinburgh: Banner of Truth Trust, 2000. 125.

i. **Owen, John**. Ed. Justin Taylor. *Overcoming Sin and Temptation.* Ed. Kelly M. Kapic. Wheaton, IL: Crossway, 2006. 53.

j. **Bunyan, John**. *Christ a Complete Saviour: Come and Welcome to Jesus Christ Justification by an Imputed Righteousness.* Teddington: Wildhern, 2007. 54.

k. **Flavel, John**. "The Fountain of Life Opened; Or, A Display of Christ in His Essential and Mediatorial Glory. Sermon VIII. Gives an Account of the Nature of Christ's Mediation." *The Whole Works of the Reverend Mr. John Flavel To Which Are Added, Alphabetical Tables of the Texts of Scripture Explained; and Indexes of the Principal Matters Contained in the Whole.* Vol. 1. London: Printed by David Gray; for J. Johnston., 1740. 48.

l. **Luther, Martin**. *Martin Luther on the Bondage of the Will. Written in Answer to the Diatribe of Erasmus on Free-Will.* Trans. Rev. Henry Cole. London: T. Bensley, 1823. 205.

m. **Gill, John**. "Book III: Of Effectual Calling." *A Complete Body of Doctrinal and Practical Divinity; Or, a System of Evangelical Truths, Deduced from the Sacred Scriptures.* Vol. 2. London, 1796. 286.

n. **Boston, Thomas**. *An Illustration of the Doctrines of the Christian Religion: With Respect to Faith and Practice, upon the Plan of the Assembly's Shorter Catechism. Comprehending a Complete Body of Divinity.* Vol. 2. Edinburgh: John Reid, 1773. 197-98.

o. **M'Cheyne, Robert Murray**. "Sermon XI 'Adoption'" *The Highway: A Repository of Historic Christianity and the Reformed Faith*. Christian Focus Publications. 27 Jan. 2012. <http://the-highway.com/MCheyne11.html>

p. **Pink, A. W**. *The Doctrine of Sanctification*. Tain: Christian Focus Publications, 2006. 211.

q. **Shelton, Jr., L. R**. "Saving Faith: Its Meaning and Its Object." *Eternal Life Ministries - Reformed/Calvinistic & Puritan Resources*. Mt. Zion Bible Church. 27 Jan. 2012. <http://www.eternallifeministries.org/lrs_faith.htm>.

r. **Calvin, John**. *Sermons on the Acts of the Apostles: Chapters 1-7*. Trans. Rob Roy McGregor. Edinburgh: Banner of Truth Trust, 2008. 28-29.

s. **Spurgeon, Charles.** "Good Works." *The Spurgeon Archive*. The Spurgeon Archive, 2001. 27 Jan. 2012. <http://www.spurgeon.org/sermons/0070.htm>.

t. **Gill, John**. *Doctrine of the Saints Final Perseverance, Asserted and Vindicated: In Answer to a Late Pamphlet, Called, Serious Thoughts, on That Subject*. London: G. Keith and J. Robinson, 1752. 3.

u. **Ryle, J. C.** *Holiness: Its Nature, Hindrances, Difficulties, and Roots*. Moscow: Charles Nolan, 2001. 149.

v. **Watson, Thomas**. *The Ten Commandments*. Edinburgh: Banner of Truth Trust, 2000. 188.

w. **Bonar, Horatius**. *God's Way of Peace: A Book for the Anxious*. London: James Nisbet and, 1864. 42-43.

x. **Pink, A. W.** *A. W. Pink's Studies in the Scriptures, 1922-1923.* Vol. 1. Sovereign Grace, 2001. 348.

y. **Ryle, J. C.** "Sabbath: A Day to Keep." *Faith Presbyterian Church Reformed of Mesquite, Texas.* 01 Nov. 2008. 27 Jan. 2012. <http:// www.fpcr.org/blue_banner_articles/ryle_sabbath.htm>.

z. **Watson, Thomas**. *The Ten Commandments.* Edinburgh: Banner of Truth Trust, 2000. 170.

aa. **Gillespie, George**. *Aaron's Rod Blossoming: Or, the Divine Ordinance of Church Government Vindicated.* Edinburgh: Robert Ogle, and Oliver & Boyd., 1844. Xvi.s

bb. **Henry, Matthew**. "Ephesians 5 – Matthew Henry Complete Commentary on the Whole Bible." *Bible Study Tools Online – Verses, Commentaries, Concordances, Verses, Parallel Versions.* 2012. 27 Jan. 2012. <http://www.biblestudytools.com/commentaries/ matthew-henry-complete/ephesians/5.html?p=3>.

cc. **Baxter, Richard**. *The Practical Works of the Late Reverend and Pious Mr. Richard Baxter.* Vol. 4. London, 1707. 661.

dd. **Owen, John**. *An Exposition of the Epistle to the Hebrews, with Preliminary Exercitations.* 2nd ed. Vol. 5. Edinburgh: J. Ritchie, 1814. 196.

ee. **Calvin, John**. *Institutes of the Christian Religion.* Trans. Henry Beveridge. Vol. 2. Edinburgh: T. & T. Clark, 1863. 624.

ff. **Gill, John**. "Baptism a Divine Commandment to Be Observed." *A Collection of Semrons and Tracts.* Vol. 2. London, 1773. 500.

gg. **Alexander, J. W**. *Remember Him*. Edinburgh: Banner of Truth Trust, 2000. 24.

hh. **Flavel, John**. "The Christian View of Death." *Grace Gems!* 27 Jan. 2012. <http://www.gracegems.org/20/Flavel_death.htm>.

ii. **Edwards, Jonathan**. *The Works of President Edwards: With a Memoir of His Life*. Vol. 6. New York: S. Converse, 1829. 412.